Famous Generals and Admirals

for Boys and Girls

by RAMON P. COFFMAN
and NATHAN G. GOODMAN

FAMOUS GENER
FOR YO

The characters for this book have been drawn from ancient as well as from modern times. Their armies and navies have fought in all parts of the world.

Some of these fighting men were moved by the desire for personal glory or gain. Others made great personal sacrifices for the good of their country. Whatever his motive or his final achievement, each man whose story is told in this book earned for himself a place among the famous fighters of history.

Alexander the Great was a conqueror at 22; Caesar managed to ferry his troops across the waters that separate France from England for the first successful invasion of that island; and Napoleon's armies at one time controlled a large part of Europe. The story of Decatur's daring exploits, the account of John Paul Jones' courageous fight and the record of Robert E. Lee's military skill and fine character are all here. Admiral Dewey, the hero of Manila Bay; General Pershing, head of the American army in France in 1917-1918, and other outstanding generals and admirals appear in this book. Once again these true stories of men of action prove that history is more exciting than fiction.

Boys and girls will find in this volume human-interest stories which furnish the clue to the fame of the characters. There are many exciting events told in the popular Coffman and Goodman style that boys and girls find so interesting.

Famous Biographies for Young People

FAMOUS VIOLINISTS FOR YOUNG PEOPLE

FAMOUS PIANISTS FOR YOUNG PEOPLE

FAMOUS COMPOSERS FOR YOUNG PEOPLE

MODERN COMPOSERS FOR YOUNG PEOPLE

FAMOUS AUTHORS FOR YOUNG PEOPLE

FAMOUS PIONEERS FOR YOUNG PEOPLE

FAMOUS EXPLORERS FOR YOUNG PEOPLE

FAMOUS GENERALS AND ADMIRALS FOR YOUNG PEOPLE

FAMOUS KINGS AND QUEENS FOR YOUNG PEOPLE

FAMOUS INVENTORS FOR YOUNG PEOPLE

FAMOUS AMERICAN POETS

FAMOUS MEN OF MEDICINE

FAMOUS WOMEN OF AMERICA

FAMOUS ENGINEERS

FAMOUS OLD MASTERS OF PAINTING

FAMOUS NATURALISTS

FAMOUS MODERN AMERICAN NOVELISTS

FAMOUS BRITISH NOVELISTS

FAMOUS BRITISH POETS

FAMOUS AMERICAN STATESMEN

FAMOUS
GENERALS AND ADMIRALS

FOR YOUNG PEOPLE

BY

RAMON PEYTON COFFMAN

AND

NATHAN G. GOODMAN

DODD, MEAD & COMPANY · NEW YORK

CONTENTS

FAMOUS GENERALS AND ADMIRALS
FOR YOUNG PEOPLE

ALEXANDER THE GREAT

ALEXANDER THE GREAT

A Conqueror At Twenty-two

BORN B.C. 356—DIED B.C. 323

To THE NORTH of ancient Greece was a country known as Macedonia. Its people were related to the Greeks, but had not made as much progress as the Greeks in art and learning.

In the year 356 B.C. the ruler of Macedonia, King Philip, had cause for great happiness. A son was born to him, and was given the name of Alexander. We are told that the delighted king, thinking of the time when the infant prince would need a teacher, wrote a letter to a friend in Athens, saying:

"This is to let you know that a son has been born to me. I am thankful to the gods, not only because of the birth of the child but also because he was born in your time. I am hoping that at some time in the future he will be your pupil, and that he will prove worthy to take my place as King of Macedonia."

The king's friend was Aristotle, and at the time was twenty-eight years old. Thirteen years later, he received another message from Philip. This time Aristotle was invited to come to the royal court to teach Prince Alexander.

The king set up buildings for a school some miles from his capital city. Here several other boys of noble birth also became pupils of Aristotle, who had become known throughout Greece as one of the famous writers and thinkers of his time. We have few records of the school days which followed, but it appears that Aristotle taught his pupils reading, writing, geometry, the poems of Homer and other subjects commonly studied in Greece.

A story, which may or may not be true, has come down concerning the

3

great teacher's prophecy about young Alexander's future. The story relates that Aristotle asked his pupils, "When you boys grow up, and take your high places in the world, what will you do for your teacher?"

One boy promised that Aristotle would be his "chief adviser," and another said, "You will always be allowed to dine at my table." Alexander, on the other hand, replied: "Why should you ask such a question? How do I know what will happen in the future? You must wait and see." At these words, Aristotle turned to the prince and said, "You have spoken well. One day you will be a really great king."

Another story about Alexander's boyhood seems true to the bold nature which showed itself in later life. On a visit to a riding field in company with his father, the twelve-year-old prince saw a number of men trying in turn to ride a black charger named Bucephalus. One after another they failed, since the animal was extremely balky and would not let any of them even mount him. The king gave orders for the horse to be taken away, but Alexander shouted, "Don't take it away! I think I can manage it!"

The king laughed, but told the youth he could try. If he failed, Alexander promised to pay the full price of the horse. The young prince turned the eyes of Bucephalus toward the sunlight. Then he leapt upon the animal's back and rode safely across the field. Tamed by the clever trick, Bucephalus became the boy's property and was his favorite for years.

The youth also was trained in the serious business of learning to be a king. Shortly before his twentieth birthday, he lost his father and found himself on the throne of Macedonia. King Philip had built up a strong army during the course of years, and this was turned over to the young king, who was very proud of the men under his command. Through his conquests of many of the cities of Greece, Philip had given his son an example which the young man seemed glad to follow. Now Alexander felt an ever-growing desire to lead his soldiers against foreign lands, and to obtain lasting power over them, one after the other.

Corinth was one of the Greek cities which had fallen under the power of Macedonia, and Alexander went there for a visit. The citizens paid him honor, and he walked through the streets feeling what a great young man he was. At length he saw a man, poorly clothed, about eighty years of age. He was told that this was the famous thinker, Diogenes. Stepping close to him, Alexander said, "I am Alexander the King."

"And I am Diogenes," replied the old man.

"Is there anything I can do for you?" asked Alexander.

"Yes, you can step aside so you won't stand between me and the sun."

That is one of the oft-told tales about Alexander, and it goes on to tell how the king turned to his comrades and remarked, "If I were not Alexander, I think I should like to be Diogenes."

Rich or poor, king or common man, Alexander probably would have found happiness in working with people. With his clear blue eyes, his curly, golden hair and his well-shaped features, he would have seemed handsome no matter what place he held in the world. Charm and physical beauty were his, as well as riches and power.

Partly because of his handsome face, but more because of his conquests, the story shortly spread that Alexander was a god. It seems there were many persons who really believed this to be true. This belief grew partly because of the ease with which Alexander made his conquests.

Having gathered an army from his own country and from Greece, the king marched into an area which then belonged to the Persian empire but which today is part of Turkey. In one of the early battles, part of Alexander's helmet was cut away by the sword of a Persian soldier. A spear, thrust through his armor covering, pierced his right shoulder. The wounded king escaped, however, and, furthermore, the battle itself was won.

During their march into Persia, the king and his men crossed the Hellespont, the narrow channel dividing Europe from a section of Asia. Today this channel is called the Dardanelles.

Although Persia lost the early battles, Darius, the Persian king, was not ready to give up his country. Hoping to crush the invaders, he formed one of the largest armies which had ever been known. We are told that it numbered a million men.

An engagement, known as the Battle of Arbela, took place on a plain near the Tigris River. Alexander had only 47,000 soldiers to face the Persian host.

Numbers, however, do not always decide a battle. The skill of a general may do a great deal to bring victory to an army which must fight a much larger one. Alexander was the skillful general to do just that. Although he was only twenty-five, he was a master in the so-called "art" of war. He knew where best to place his foot-soldiers with their long pikes, where best to send his 7,000 cavalry charging with their spears.

The Persians had 200 chariots and these were driven furiously toward the Macedonians. Each chariot had a long blade at either side, a blade which could cut down men as a scythe cuts tall grass. Alexander gave orders to his soldiers to seize the bridles of the advancing horses! Fearlessly they carried out his command and the armed chariots did little damage.

Alexander's men won the Battle of Arbela and the Persians were put to flight.

The victorious king then turned his attention to other lands to conquer. Among the cities which Alexander wanted to capture was one named Tyre, the capital of ancient Phoenicia. Tyre was important because of its fleet. Alexander believed that if he captured the city, he would obtain its war galleys, and would be able to use them in an attack on Egypt.

Situated on a little island about three-quarters of a mile from the mainland, Tyre was not an easy city to capture. Since Alexander had few ships of his own, he had to find some way of getting there with his army.

A bold idea came to him. Why not build a roadway to the island! Fortunately, the water was shallow. He set thousands of his men to work, and even labored with his own hands. As the weeks and months passed, the road, or causeway, grew longer and longer. Stones, tree trunks and soil were used in building it.

From time to time, war galleys from Tyre were rowed out and showers of arrows were shot at the workers. To save his men from these attacks, Alexander ordered large wooden screens to be set up and moved forward as the laborers pressed ahead.

After several months of work, the causeway reached a point a few hundred feet from the edge of the island. Using catapults behind the great wall of their city, the Tyrians now hurled hot sand at the enemy. The sand came in

6

clouds, choking and almost blinding those who were struck by it. The hot sand was something like poison gas in modern warfare.

Large wooden towers built by Alexander's men were made ready with battering rams to be used against the city wall. From time to time, these towers were set afire by fire-darts, but Alexander's men put out each blaze as the towers were shoved closer and closer.

Meanwhile Alexander had obtained a number of war galleys from the island of Cyprus, and from several cities to the north which had agreed to accept his rule. These galleys proved extremely helpful in the siege. The bold attackers at length made a breach in the city wall, and pushed through it with their leader in the thickest part of the battle. There were those who said that Alexander had a "charmed life." Often he appeared where the fighting was hardest, and sometimes he was wounded, but each time he escaped with his life.

Tyre finally fell into his hands, and 30,000 of the people were sold into slavery, in the year which we call 332 B.C.

Now the way to Egypt had been made ready. Alexander the Great, as he is known in history, obtained an easy victory in Egypt. In fact, after capturing one of the cities near the border, he was given a hearty welcome by the Egyptians.

Before the coming of Alexander, Egypt had been a part of the Persian empire. The people did not like Persian rule and seemed to believe they would be better treated by the young conqueror from the north.

In the city of Memphis, he visited the temples and paid honor to the Egyptian gods. This increased the favor with which he was looked upon in the land of the Nile, a country with a long history even in those early days.

Alexander laid out a new city for the Egyptians. He planned to have it settled by Greeks and expected it to become a great center of trade for his empire. The city was, in fact, destined to live and grow for centuries under the name of Alexandria. Today it is Egypt's greatest seaport.

Leaving Egypt, Alexander took his army in a northeasterly direction. Without needing to lay siege to it, he entered the ancient city of Babylon. By this time, he had come to believe that it was, indeed, his fate to conquer the

7

world. He had little idea of the true size of the earth, but he intended to possess as much of its surface as possible.

His next drive was eastward toward India. It was a long, hard journey, much of the way across high and difficult mountains. India was reached at last, and the border crossed. The young leader would have liked to conquer the entire country, but his men began to complain about the hardships they were having to go through. Therefore the general turned back to Persia with his army, after founding another new city, also called Alexandria, near India's border.

Once more he took up quarters in Babylon, and this time decided to make it the capital of his whole empire. Unhappily for him, the glory of his rule as emperor in Babylon was to be short lived. After taking part in a great deal of feasting and revelry, he fell ill with a fever. Eleven days later, he died.

Alexander the Great was only thirty-three when he died, but in his short life he had built a huge empire through his skill on the battlefield and his boldness as a ruler. The empire, however, did not last long after the death of its founder. It was divided, placed under the power of several rulers, and before long fell to pieces.

HANNIBAL

HANNIBAL

North Africa to Italy

BORN B.C. 247—DIED B.C. 183

N<small>EXT TO EGYPT</small>, Tunisia is the most important part of northern Africa. It is less than one hundred miles from Sicily, and Sicily is separated from Italy by the Strait of Messina, only two miles wide. Tunisia and Sicily were both occupied by American and British troops in 1943.

Tunisia's history stretches back many centuries. The city of Carthage, famous in ancient times, was in this region before it was called Tunisia. That celebrated city was situated only a few miles from Tunis, the present capital of Tunisia. The settlers had come from the country which the Romans called Phoenicia. The ancient Hebrews called it Canaan.

Within three centuries after it was founded, Carthage had power over a number of islands, as well as over some land in northern Africa. Among the islands ruled by Carthage were Sardinia, Corsica, Malta and a part of Sicily.

The people of Carthage were largely seamen and merchants. Their vessels sailed far and wide over the Mediterranean Sea, carrying goods to and from Spain and other parts of southern Europe.

The names of some of the leaders of Carthage offer a hint as to the religion of the people. Two generals were named Hasdrubal and Hannibal. The meaning of Hasdrubal is "one who trusts in Baal." Hannibal means "favored by Baal."

Baal was worshiped as an important god. He was said to rule the bright

11

sun. Another god of Carthage was supposed to have a cruel nature, and was known as Moloch. Children sometimes were offered to him as sacrifice.

In history we read about the Punic wars. The name Punic came from the Latin language, and its meaning is the same as Carthaginian.

The Carthaginian, or Punic, wars were fought between Carthage and Rome. They lasted for 118 years. There were of course periods of peace, but there were forty-three years of actual fighting during the three main wars which took place.

One of the chief characters in the story of the Punic wars was Hannibal. He was, indeed, one of the most skillful generals in all history. He it was who led the armies of Carthage in the Second Punic war which lasted from 218 to 201 B.C.

The father of Hannibal also was a general and an enemy of Rome. Legend says that Hannibal, as an eight-year-old boy, was told to swear that he would treat Rome as an enemy all through his life. The order, it was said, came from his father.

Whether or not the legend is true, it is certain that Hannibal was told many unpleasant things about Rome during his boyhood. Much of his time during that period was spent with soldiers from whom he learned the ways of war. When he reached young manhood, he considered himself a soldier whose duty it was to make war on Rome.

The Romans, on their side, were bitter enemies of Carthage. They wanted to spread their power over Spain and over the part of Africa now called Tunisia. Carthage, which had been a center of sea power, stood in their way.

The Romans had shown less skill in sea fighting than in land fighting. In battles on land, the Romans usually came out victors. There was a question whether the soldiers of Carthage would dare to challenge Rome on the continent of Europe.

Would the Carthaginians stay in their homeland because of fear, or would they strike across the sea? Would they wait, perhaps, until Rome built up complete control of the sea?

Hannibal was the man who was to answer those questions. At the age of twenty-five, following his father's death, he became the chief general of

Carthage. Almost as soon as he took control of his country's army, he started the first steps of a drive on Rome. He struck through Spain, and marched with his soldiers in the direction of northern Italy.

What an odd sight a "panzer" division of ancient Carthage would seem today! It was made up of armored elephants instead of armored tanks!

Hannibal, leader of the army of Carthage, had a limited force of these live tanks. There were only thirty-seven elephants, but they were expected to serve well when battles with the Romans took place.

Hannibal finally reached the western bank of the Rhone River. In addition to his elephants, he had with him 90,000 foot soldiers and 12,000 cavalry. The crossing of the Rhone proved to be a task that required much skill and planning. The enemy had drawn up an army on the other side, but Hannibal knew how to meet hard tasks and master them. Secretly he sent some of his soldiers upstream a few miles, and ordered them to cross the river and surprise the enemy by striking from the rear. The orders were carried out, and the crossing was made.

Next the Carthaginians faced a far stronger bar to their progress, the dangerous mountain passes of the Alps. Hannibal ordered his troops forward, and forward they went. They struggled upward, elephants and all, toward the narrow passes and through into Italy The crossing took fifteen days. Each day many of the invaders lost their lives. Some died from cold, and others were victims of hostile men who attacked them in the mountains. Huge boulders were rolled down on them by their enemies who were guarding the passes.

The heavy losses in crossing the Alps might have made another general decide that his cause was lost. Not so with Hannibal! His confidence in his own skill in warfare was strong enough to carry him on even though he had lost many thousands of soldiers.

There was good reason, however, for Hannibal to expect some help. In Italy lived hundreds of thousands of people who did not like the Roman rule. Men from many districts might be counted on to join an invading army.

So it turned out. Thousands of Gauls in northern Italy joined Hannibal. More thousands were added to his army as he marched through the central

13

and southern parts of the peninsula. Again and again they helped him in battle.

More than once, Hannibal met Roman armies which were larger than his own, but he defeated them one after another. Often his supplies were low, but he kept on fighting.

Of his many battles in Italy, one of the most important is known as the Battle of Cannae. It was named after Cannae, an ancient town in southern Italy near which it was fought in 216 B.C.

There is a difference of opinion as to the exact numbers on the two sides, but all accounts agree that Hannibal had fewer soldiers. His total force probably was no more than 50,000. Against him were about 85,000 Romans.

Hannibal, however, had a far larger cavalry force than the Romans, about 10,000 mounted men against 6,000. Before the battle was very old, the Roman cavalry was put to flight, and then Hannibal closed a trap on the infantry. When the fighting ended that day, almost all the Roman foot soldiers were dead.

After his many victories, it seems strange that Hannibal did not attack and capture Rome. At one time he moved close to the capital of the Roman empire, but failed to place it under siege. The chief reason given is that Hannibal was without machines of war of the type then used to capture walled cities. Another reason offered is that Hannibal's army was too small to surround such a large city.

In any case the failure to capture Rome meant the failure of Hannibal's long campaign. He spent fifteen years in Italy, and his army was slowly worn down. Many of the soldiers, especially those whose bodies had been weakened by years of fighting, were anxious to return home. A few thousand soldiers were sent from Carthage, but otherwise little help came from home. For the most part, Hannibal and his soldiers had to live from the country. His brother, Hasdrubal, tried to bring in a new army from Spain, but was defeated on the way and lost his life.

Toward the end of Hannibal's invasion of Italy, a young Roman general named Scipio started to turn the tide of war against Carthage. He led an army of invaders into the part of Africa now known as Tunisia. Fearing that their capital city would be captured, the leaders at Carthage sent orders to Hannibal to come home at once. With great skill he placed his troops aboard sailing vessels and crossed the Mediterranean back to Carthage.

Upon his return, Hannibal led an army against Scipio, but this time he was defeated. His force was conquered by Scipio at Zama in 202 B.C. It was the only important battle Hannibal lost in his long career, but it was a most serious defeat. Carthage lost the war and was forced to pay tribute to Rome.

Hannibal fled to the eastern end of the Mediterranean Sea where he was given protection. He died at the age of sixty-four.

JULIUS CAESAR

JULIUS CAESAR

First to Invade Britain

BORN B.C. 100—DIED B.C. 44

UNTIL THE END of the first World War, there were men in power in Europe with titles which could be traced back to ancient Rome. There were, for example, the Czar—or "Caesar"—of Russia and the Kaiser of Germany. "Kaiser" is the German form of "Caesar." The emperors of ancient Rome were known as Caesars.

The man whose name brought this title into being never actually wore a crown. He was Julius Caesar, and he lived 2,000 years ago.

Julius Caesar is believed to have been born in the year we call 100 B.C. The Romans, of course, had no "B.C.'s" in their calendar system.

Although his family was well-to-do, Caesar in his youth began to take an interest in the welfare of the common people, known at that time as "plebs." His interest may have sprung from the teachings of a slave from Gaul, who helped to give him his early education. This man knew how to speak both Greek and Latin. He may have told young Caesar about the wrongs which the Gauls had suffered under Roman rule.

One of the uncles of Julius Caesar was the noted Marius, a general who was on the side of the plebs against the wealthy patricians. For a time Marius was the most powerful Roman leader, but his army at length was defeated by one led by Sulla.

After winning an important victory, Sulla came back to Rome in triumph. Friends of Marius were hunted down, and Caesar, now a young man, came close to losing his life. We are told that the Vestal Virgins, the honored priest-esses who kept bright the holy fire of the city, made a plea to save him. He was not put to death, but his property was taken from him and he thought it best to leave Rome. The next three years he spent at the eastern end of the Mediterranean Sea, serving with the Roman Army. During that time he took part in efforts to stamp out bands of pirates who had been taking a toll of Roman sailing vessels.

When word came to him that Sulla was dead, he quickly returned home. Soon afterward he was elected to an office in which he helped watch over the grain supply of Rome, also over public works. Later he was chosen as a praetor, an officer whose duties were similar to those of a judge in a modern law court.

The next step in Caesar's rise to power was his appointment to the office of governor of the province of Spain. This position took him away from home again, but he enjoyed traveling and was glad to have the rich rewards which came from his new office. Much of the money he obtained at this time was used to pay his debts. The debts had grown partly because he had given free public shows and had paid for them with borrowed money. It was a custom in those days to win favor by giving people in Rome free seats to watch circus performers and gladiators.

When he came back to Rome, Caesar took pains to form a friendship with Crassus, a very rich man. The fortune of Crassus amounted to about $10,000,-000, and he was probably the richest man in the city. At one time he gave a feast for all citizens who cared to come, and the food was served on 10,000 tables!

Caesar also became a close friend of Pompey, a general who had won success on the battlefield and had held the office of consul. Thanks to this friendship, and to that of Crassus, Caesar was chosen as one of the two consuls of Rome.

Caesar was now about forty-one years of age. He had been married in his early manhood, but his wife had died seven years before he became consul, leaving him a daughter who, at this time, was growing into young woman-hood. Partly to help his career, Caesar now married a relative of Pompey's.

Brutus, a young Roman who was to rise in politics, had asked for the hand of Julia, the daughter of Caesar, and the promise had been given. Caesar, however, broke the promise and allowed Pompey to marry Julia. Thus he became the father-in-law of a man six years older than himself! The broken promise might have played a part in causing Brutus to commit a tragic deed at the close of Caesar's life.

At the time of Pompey's marriage to Caesar's daughter, Caesar, Pompey and Crassus held almost all the power in the Roman republic. It seemed, at first, that they might always be united as rulers, but fortune was to make the story turn out otherwise.

After serving his term as consul, Caesar was given command of the Roman legions in Gaul, a land which covered almost the same area as present-day France. There he spent ten years, much of it engaged in fighting against Teutonic or German tribesmen, and against certain tribes of Gauls which rose in rebellion. In almost every battle and skirmish, the Romans were victorious.

During the years in which he was in control of Gaul, Caesar made two invasions of Britain. Roman legions, in 55 B.C., for the first time trod on the soil of the island now known as Great Britain. Later they camped where the huge city of London was to rise. These invasions pointed the way for Roman soldiers to come later and occupy Britain. Rome held it for four centuries.

While he was in Gaul, Caesar made notes about the many problems he had to meet there and about the battles which were fought. These notes were to be used in preparing a book on the subject. Millions of boys and girls have studied Caesar's writings in their Latin classes in high school.

In his own story it is seen that Caesar was a great leader, but shortly before his time of command in Gaul was to run out, he received strange word from Rome. Plans had been made to take his troops from him and to make him once more merely a private citizen!

During his long absence from Rome, his daughter Julia had died. His rich friend Crassus had gone at the head of an army to conquer the Parthians, and had been captured and put to death. Pompey had grown jealous of Caesar, and had been working to make himself the chief ruler of Rome.

21

At this point, Caesar decided to strike fast and hard. At the head of his loyal soldiers, he crossed a stream on the border of Gaul and entered Italy. The stream was the Rubicon, and we have today the expression "crossing the Rubicon," meaning that we take an important step from which we cannot turn back.

As he moved forward, Caesar gained strength, more and more soldiers joining his army. When reports came to Pompey about Caesar's approach, he did not feel that his army was strong enough to meet Caesar on the battlefield. He therefore took what soldiers he could gather and hurried across the Adriatic Sea to Greece, where he was able to muster thousands of additional men.

It seemed plain that there could be no peace in the empire so long as Pompey had an army. Caesar now started in hot pursuit. In an early battle he was defeated, but was able to make a retreat with most of his soldiers. A friend gathered for him several thousand additional soldiers, and soon he was ready to attack Pompey near Pharsalus, a town in northern Greece.

In the Battle of Pharsalus, Pompey had 57,000 foot soldiers and 7,000 cavalrymen. On his side Caesar had only 24,000 men, most of them foot-soldiers. Caesar, however, planned and fought the battle so cleverly that he put Pompey's men to rout, capturing 24,000 of them. During the fighting, Caesar's foot-soldiers dared to drive into the enemy cavalry, striking with their swords and spears at both horses and riders.

Pompey escaped to Egypt, but there he was murdered. Thus Julius Caesar was left master of the Roman empire. It was an empire which kept some of the old forms of the republic, but the real power was in one man's hands. Caesar became "dictator for life."

There was a legend in Caesar's family that one of its founders had been the goddess Venus. After the winning of his many victories, Julius Caesar seems to have come to believe that he himself was a god, a god who was on earth for the purpose of ruling a mighty empire. A statue of him was set up in a temple at Rome, and carved on it were the words, "To the Unconquerable God." His image was carried in a procession, along with the images of old Roman deities.

While in power, Caesar changed the old Roman calendar, which had failed to keep the months in the proper seasons. For many centuries loose ways of figuring the length of the year had been followed. The ruler now ordered that one year should have fifteen months, so the calendar could catch up with the seasons. He also provided a better plan for counting time in the future.

The Julian Calendar, as it was called, was not perfect, but it was the best one the Romans had ever had. One month in the new calendar was called July in honor of Caesar. It came from his name, Julius.

In his other public acts as dictator, Caesar was for the most part just and, at times, kindly. Yet there were Romans who felt that no one person should take so much power to himself. These men banded together in a plot, and on a given signal attacked Caesar and stabbed him, leaving him dying. One of those who carried out the plot was Marcus Brutus, who years before had hoped to marry Caesar's daughter. He had fought for Pompey at Pharsalus, but had been pardoned by Caesar after the fighting was over.

The death of Caesar took place when he was about fifty-five years of age, only three years after the Battle of Pharsalus. The assassination ended the life of a dictator, but never again was Rome to be a real republic. New dictators were to arise, fighting among themselves for power; and there was started a line of emperors who called themselves "Caesars."

Julius Caesar ranks high among the generals of ancient times. Although less brilliant than Alexander or Hannibal, he probably was the most able leader ever to stand at the head of Roman armies.

WILLIAM THE CONQUEROR

WILLIAM THE CONQUEROR

He Invaded England

BORN 1027 (?)—DIED 1087

IN WESTERN FRANCE, a few miles from the coast of the English Channel, is the little city of Bayeux. It has a population of only about 7,000, but it is more than a thousand years old. The people of Bayeux make excellent lace and are also noted for their chinaware, but the place is best known as the home of the Bayeux Tapestry.

The Bayeux Tapestry is a long strip of cloth with pictures which tell the story of the Norman conquest of England. The cloth is brownish linen, only twenty inches wide but 230 feet long. The pictures were sewed, or embroidered, on the cloth with woolen thread or yarn. Blue, green, yellow, red, black and buff threads were used to work in the figures of men, animals, boats and buildings.

The men shown are kings, nobles, knights and foot-soldiers. Among them are King Edward the Confessor and King Harold of England, also Duke William and Bishop Odo of Normandy.

Bishop Odo once held sway over Bayeux and it is believed that the tapestry was made for use in his cathedral there. No one knows who sewed the figures on the tapestry, but one legend says that the work was done by Queen Matilda, wife of William the Conqueror.

There are seventy-two scenes, making a picture-story. Harold is shown as he is saying good-bye to King Edward, taking a boat to France, and being made prisoner by a French earl. Later, Harold is seen taking an oath that

27

he will not attempt to interfere with William's effort to gain the English throne.

Harold, however, did not keep this promise. He let himself be crowned King of England. This action led Duke William to prepare to invade England with as large an army as he could muster. The tapestry gives us views of Normans cutting trees and building boats for the invasion.

The Bayeux Tapestry was not woven in the way tapestries are usually made, and the figures are rather crude, but it is of more value than any other piece of cloth in the world.

William, the leading figure in this tapestry, was a man of great importance. He was known as Duke William and was master of a section of France called Normandy. Men of the North, sea rovers known as Vikings or Norsemen, had settled in this part of France more than a century and a half before. They had accepted the ways of the French, and had learned to speak the French language. People spoke of them as the Normans.

In England, at the time, there lived Britons, Angles, Saxons and Danes. The Angles and Saxons were the ruling group, their ancestors having come from Germany six centuries before. The name "England" arose from "Angle-land." The Britons, however, were members of a race which had been on the island for thousands of years. They had married with the Angles and Saxons to a large extent and had merged with them as Anglo-Saxons.

The Danes, on the other hand, were newcomers. They were masters over some parts of England, but had not mixed very much with the other people in the country. They were of Norse stock but were not friendly with the Normans.

Since Duke William wanted to be King of England, he gathered an army which was large for those days, though it probably did not number more than 40,000 soldiers and knights. It was made up of Normans, Frenchmen and others. Their chief weapons were spears, swords, and bows and arrows. Many of the men were almost covered with coats-of-mail.

It was in the year 1066 that the Normans embarked to cross the choppy waters of the English Channel. Duke William's vessel was the fastest in the fleet, and sailed so far ahead of the others that it had to drop its sails to give them time to catch up. When the landing was made, there was not a single English soldier on the shore to bar the way.

As he stepped from his boat, Duke William tripped and almost fell. We are told that those around him groaned as they saw him stumble, saying, "This is a bad omen." William, however, gained his feet and shouted: "No, it is a good omen! Do you see this soil in my hand? It is proof that I shall own all the land of England!"

As he spoke, he opened his hand to show his men the sand which he had picked up from the beach. It was a custom of the time to give soil to a person who bought land. Duke William, however, was not buying England. He planned to take it!

The battle to decide who should own England was fought six miles from a little town called Hastings and is commonly known to this day as the Battle of Hastings, although it also has been spoken of as the Battle of Senlac Hill.

The fighting took place on an October day in 1066, two weeks and two days after the landing of Duke William and his Normans.

To meet the invaders, King Harold had brought to the south of England an army composed entirely of foot-soldiers. With battle-axes, swords and spears, the English ranged themselves around the upper parts of Senlac Hill. Behind them was a forest.

The Normans were divided into bands of foot-soldiers, archers and cavalry, before they set forth to climb the hill and drive the English back.

The arrows shot by Norman archers had little effect, at first, since the English held their shields together in long rows, and warded off the missiles. When the Norman foot-soldiers advanced, they were struck down by blows from English battle-axes. Some of them turned to run away, and a number of English soldiers ran after them. Then the Norman cavalry crashed forward and slew those of the English who had broken their ranks.

This situation gave Duke William an idea. Later in the battle he ordered a large number of his foot-soldiers to retreat. Again the English broke their ranks in pursuit and again were cut down, this time in large numbers.

Some of the English remained on the hill, however, and to master them, the duke ordered his archers to shoot upward so that arrows would rain down

29

on the heads of the foe. This trick did much to defeat the English Army. King Harold himself fell, mortally wounded. The small number of his soldiers who were not slain or wounded ran to cover in the forest. Duke William and his men had won the day.

The victory gave Duke William power over southern England. After reaching London, he was crowned king. The event took place on Christmas Day, 1066.

Within a few years, the new king made himself master of all England. He came to be called "William the Conqueror."

William and the Normans did more than win political power over England. They also took the land away from those who had owned it. Norman lords were given estates which had belonged to nobles of Anglo-Saxon or Danish blood. King William made up an excuse for taking the land. He declared that those who had fought against him were traitors, since they had opposed the rightful king. For himself, he took the lands which Harold had owned, and much more besides. He gave earldoms to his relatives and friends. Bishop Odo was made an earl, and was granted land in seventeen counties. Later in his life, however, Odo fell from royal favor, and was thrown into prison.

King William ordered a record to be made of all the lands and livestock in England. This report, in two large volumes, came to be known as the "Domesday Book."

Concerning this census, an old English writer declared: "The king sent over all England and had it made out how many hundred hides were in each shire, and what the king himself had in lands and livestock on the lands. Also he had written how much land was owned by his archbishops, bishops, abbots and earls and how much money it might be worth. There was not one single hide of land, nor even, it is a shame to say, one ox or cow or hog that was not set down in the record." King William was pleased when he saw this list of properties.

At the time of the Battle of Hastings, William the Conqueror had not yet reached his fortieth birthday. From that time until his death he was to be King of England, and his son and grandson were also to rule as kings of the country he had won.

More than once the people in one part of England or another rose in revolt, but each time they were put down by William's soldiers. In 1087, when he was close to sixty years of age, King William left England and took part in an invasion of France. His troops were successful in capturing the enemy town of Mantes. By his order the town was burned, and later he rode through the streets to look at the ruins. Suddenly his horse was startled by the touch of a hot cinder and lurched forward. William was thrown against the pommel of his saddle and was hurt so badly that he died shortly afterward.

William the Conqueror brought a ruling group of Normans into England. He also gave England a new interest in the continent of Europe, and a claim to Normandy. Later kings were to enlarge the claims, and much warfare was to take place between England and France in the following centuries.

JENGHIZ KHAN

JENGHIZ KHAN

He Built a Vast Empire

BORN 1162 (?)—DIED 1227

Turning back the pages of history, one finds a number of conquerors who have upset the world. One of these was Jenghiz Khan. Another spelling of the first part of the name is Genghis. In either case the way to pronounce it is "jengiz." The word "khan" means "lord" or "prince."

Jenghiz was born in 1162, almost a century after William the Conqueror invaded England. The tribe in which he was born lived in a part of Asia made up largely of mountains. The climate in that part of the world is cold, and life was hard for the wandering Mongols.

The men in the tribe were experts at riding their sure-footed ponies. This knowledge of horses was to prove useful in the later sweep of conquest.

As a boy of only thirteen, Jenghiz became the chief of his tribe! During his young manhood, he led his warriors into battle against nearby tribes. For over twenty years he met with success in most of these fights, but his main conquests did not start until after he was forty years old.

At the age of forty, on one occasion, his power was nearly wiped out. In warfare with Wang Khan, leader of the tribesmen known as Keraits, his army was cut to pieces. With only a small band of his men, he escaped, fleeing to the desert.

If Jenghiz had lost his life in that conflict, what a difference it would have made in future history! How many thousands of unhappy men, women and children would have been saved!

35

As it was, he escaped death and gathered a new army. Then began the real conquest of the world's largest continent. The Keraits were beaten down, and their lands were added to those which the Mongol lord already ruled.

The next few years were spent in a southwestward drive against the Turks, many of whom then lived in the center of Asia. Their country was laid waste. Another campaign was carried out against the Chinese in northern China. This, also, was successful and Jenghiz Khan became the master of more land and more people.

When the vast conquests of Jenghiz Khan are studied, it is easy to see that he could not have made them without hardy, well-trained soldiers. His Mongol tribesmen had lived in the saddle from boyhood, and were skillful riders. In those days—more than seven centuries ago—all long and rapid journeys had to be made on the backs of such animals as the Mongolian ponies which the men of Jenghiz rode.

Jenghiz himself was a strong leader. He knew how to make ready for battle. He was cool-headed and crafty. He was cruel of heart, and did not care how much he made people suffer so long as he could add to his personal power and glory.

Jenghiz knew how to make total war. When he sent his army through a new country, scenes of horror were left behind him. Homes were burned to the ground, and the people themselves were killed by the thousands.

This plan of laying waste the country was not followed just because the Mongol leader wanted to be cruel. He had, in fact, another very important purpose. After becoming the ruler of so much land, he feared that the conquered cities might later rise in revolt, and it seemed safer to destroy the cities as he captured them. In that way he could be assured against rebellions in his rear.

Many of the peasants who were captured were not put to death. Instead they were made to dig trenches and perform other tasks which needed to be done before an attack was begun on a strongly defended city. Then, when the attack was made, the peasants often were driven in front of the Mongol soldiers. With their bodies they stopped the enemy's arrows and darts, and thus saved the lives of many of the Khan's fighting men. If they happened to escape the arrows and darts, they were crowded forward until they were struck by the spears or swords of the defenders of the city.

In this manner Jenghiz Khan carried on his sweeping conquests, most of them being made during the last fourteen years of his life. He was fifty-one years old when he marched with a mighty army to invade northern China. This area was then in the hands of hard-fighting Tartars. They were defeated in several battles. A breach was made in the Great Wall, and the Mongols swarmed ahead to high cliffs in the province of Shantung.

In the conquest of northern China, Jenghiz had personal charge of the center of his army. Three of his sons commanded the right wing, and three of his brothers led the left wing. All three sections of the army were victorious.

In later years a great part of central and southern China came under the sway of the Mongol ruler. Hundreds of cities and millions of people were added to his empire.

Before completing the conquest of China, Jenghiz sent troops in several other directions. Sometimes he went with them himself, but at other times he sent generals, usually his relatives, on long expeditions.

Jenghiz and one of his sons rode more than 3,000 miles from their Mongolian home almost to the eastern side of the Caspian Sea. On their way they had to fight the Turks as well as the armies of other lands through which they passed. The Turks lost many of their cities. Thousands of their people were killed and other thousands fled to Asia Minor. Their homeland had been in central Asia, but they left it in terror of the Mongols. The later invasion of southeastern Europe by the Turks was largely a result of their having been driven back years before by Jenghiz Khan.

One of the important battles against the Turks took place in northern India, on the banks of the Indus River. Although the Turks were outnumbered, they fought bravely. Seeing that his cause was lost, Jelal ed-Din, the Turkish leader, turned his horse, and horse and rider leapt into the river from the top of a cliff twenty feet high. Then the horse swam to the other side, and Jelal ed-Din escaped by riding to Delhi.

Jenghiz himself never set foot in Europe, but he sent an army there. Pushing through what is now known as European Russia, the Mongols reached the Dnieper River. Envoys were sent to Russian princes in command of an army near the city of Kiev. The envoys were put to death by the princes, and a battle soon followed. The Russians, however, were badly defeated, and those who did not die on the battlefield turned and fled for their lives.

Instead of trying to hold the land around the Dnieper, the Mongols gathered what booty they could carry and turned back toward their homeland. They had killed scores of thousands of men, women and children during this raid, in which they made their farthest advance to the west.

Meanwhile Jenghiz Khan had returned to his capital and was trying to enjoy his power, but now and then he found it necessary to go forth to punish some province which had risen in rebellion. He was returning from an excursion into central Asia when he gazed into the sky at night and saw several planets unusually close together. He pondered over what he saw and took this as a sign that ill fortune would come to him. It was shortly afterward that he fell sick and died.

The scores of victories which had been won under his leadership gave Jenghiz power, of a sort, from the China Sea to the Dnieper River, but most of this vast empire fell to pieces after his death. His grandson, Kublai Khan, later obtained a firm control over China, or Cathay, but he never made any attempt to invade Europe.

FREDERICK THE GREAT

FREDERICK THE GREAT

The Prussian Army

BORN 1712—DIED 1786

FOR CENTURIES, Prussia has been the center of German power. It is the part of Germany in which Berlin is located. Close to two centuries ago, Prussia set out to conquer other parts of Europe and in that way to build an empire.

Going back 1,500 years, we find the early German tribes swarming into southern Europe. They conquered Italy, France, Spain, Portugal and other lands. At that time, they were called barbarians by people of the old Roman empire.

When the German tribes went southward, they deserted parts of their old homeland, leaving behind few, if any, residents. One such district was south of the Baltic Sea, and that is where Prussia was later to grow.

Tribes of Slavs moved into the unoccupied lands. These people were of the same race as the Poles and Russians.

The Germans conquered the south of Europe, but not all of them stayed there. Many returned to the lands in the north where they had lived before, but found the Slavs there. After making war against them, the Germans drove out most of the Slavs and reoccupied their old lands.

For a long time, these lands south of the Baltic Sea were ruled by nobles. Some of them were Germans; others were Poles. In 1707 one of these noblemen founded what he called the Kingdom of Prussia. His name was Frederick, and he became the first king of Prussia.

To his son, Frederick William, may be given most of the credit or blame for starting Prussia in its pursuit of military power and the development of well-trained armies. His father had left him an army of 27,000 men, and he soon took steps to enlarge it. Before he died, his army numbered 50,000 soldiers. Some nations in Europe had larger armies, but Frederick William's soldiers were outstanding because they were so well-drilled. Prussian drill-masters got results. They barked commands at their troops, and the troops obeyed on the instant.

Frederick William's ideas of military conquest helped to bring about the formation and growth of the German empire many years later. One of his hobbies was to search for tall men to serve as soldiers. He gathered them in very much the same way a person collects postage stamps in these modern days. He called his tall soldiers "Lange Jungen," which means "Tall Boys" or "Long Boys."

In his palace, however, all was not peaceful. The king thought that a man should live the life of a soldier, but his wife, the queen, was interested in books and loved the polite manners for which the French were noted. She knew the French language and spoke it almost as well as if she had been a Frenchwoman.

The king would have pardoned such interests on the part of his wife if it had not been for his son. He wanted the boy to grow up a soldier like himself. He was hardly pleased, therefore, when a French governess was chosen for the little Prince Frederick.

The boy learned French and liked to speak it much better than German. He said that the German language was dull, and for years he called his French governess "mamma."

A Frenchman was chosen as tutor for the prince when he grew too old to be under the care of a governess. One of the things Prince Frederick learned was how to play the flute. The king did not change his son's education until it was too late to keep the boy from forming his taste for the French language and French manners.

"Am I to have a French-speaking, flute-playing son?" he asked at last. "No! I will make a soldier of him!"

At the age of fifteen, Prince Frederick was given military training, and was allowed to ride at the head of a company of the Tall Boys his father had gathered from many parts of Europe.

"He must get French and English ways out of his head," said the king. "He must do just what I tell him to do!"

The prince did not like this sudden change in his training. Angered by things his father said to him, he at length decided to run away. So, at the age of seventeen, in company with a friend, he left the palace. They entered a waiting stagecoach and drove off, but were caught before they could go very far.

"My son has tried to desert the army!" stormed the king. "He shall be punished!"

A hard fate met the youth who had joined Prince Frederick in this attempt to escape from the palace. By order of the king, he was put to death. The life of the prince was spared, but for some time he was kept under close guard.

In the years which followed, the prince was in close touch with the Army. At the age of twenty we find him writing a letter which showed that he had changed some of his ideas. It contained these words:

"I have just drilled, and I shall keep on drilling. I would rather drill here from dawn to dusk than live as a rich man in Berlin!"

A year later came Frederick's wedding day. On order of the king, he was married to the niece of the Austrian emperor. He did not love her, but he was afraid to stand against his father's will.

The years passed, and Frederick worked faithfully with the Army. At length he was given the rank of colonel. As he grew older, the ideas of his youth changed more and more. He did not entirely give up his love for books, but his mind became filled with the idea of great military power. He looked forward to the time when he would become king, and he dreamed of adding more land to his kingdom.

Drill, drill, drill! That was the way of Prussia. Her soldiers were perhaps the best-trained in all Europe. Frederick's father died in 1740, when the prince was twenty-eight years old; and he found himself on the throne of Prussia. He soon added to the size of his army, and before long 90,000 men were on its rolls.

As king, he ruled under the name of Frederick II. To the world he became known as "Frederick the Great," but some persons declare he does not deserve the title of "Great."

Frederick had enemies, and we are told that at one time an effort was made to poison him. It is said that he was making ready to drink a cup of coffee when a sentry rushed into the room and stood close to him at attention.

"Are you crazy?" asked Frederick. "Why did you come bursting into my study?"

"My king," replied the sentry. "I saw a man enter this room and put something in your coffee. It may have been poison!" The story goes on to say that the coffee was tested and was, indeed, found to contain poison. Following a strict rule of the Army, the sentry had not dared to speak until the king asked him a question.

Frederick's reign was a long one, lasting almost half a century. He early displayed his faith in force and did not hesitate to make war on his neighbors so he could add to the size and power of his kingdom. He built up a much larger and stronger army than his father had left him, and he used this army to win an empire.

In 1740, the first year of his rule as king, he made war against Austria, at that time a country of considerable size. He sent a declaration of war, but struck the first blow before his message had had time to reach the Austrian capital.

The war lasted a year and a half and, as a result, Frederick obtained a part of Austria. Two years later, he fought another war against Austria, and again he added to the land under his rule.

Declaring that he feared an attack of revenge by Austria, Frederick struck a third time. This new war is known in history as the Seven Years' War. The Prussians lost some battles, but won victories as well. At the end of the fighting, Prussia stood out as one of the leading powers of Europe.

All through his reign, Frederick maintained that he was working for the good of his people. That is a point about which we cannot be sure. The Prussians were forced into the Army by the thousands. New soldiers were continually taking the places of those who had died on the field of battle. The size of the Prussian Army was raised to 200,000, a vast number for those days.

In 1772, Frederick carried out a bold and ruthless plan to split the kingdom of Poland into several parts. One section, went to Russia, another to Austria, and a third to himself. By that raid alone he added 13,000 square miles to the lands in his empire. In later years, after Frederick was dead, the rest of Poland was gobbled up and wiped from the map. Not until 1919, after the close of the first World War, did the Polish nation obtain independence again.

Frederick died at Postdam, Germany, on August 17, 1786. He had been ruler of Prussia for forty-six years.

GEORGE WASHINGTON

GEORGE WASHINGTON

First in War and Peace

BORN 1732—DIED 1799

Old family bibles often contain odd but valuable notes on the front and back pages. Sometimes one finds a list of relatives with the dates of their births, including the hour of the day at which children in the family were born. In the Washington family Bible at Mount Vernon, Virginia, there is this entry: "George Washington, son to Augustine and Mary, his wife, was born ye 11th day of February about 10 in the morning and was baptized the 5th of April following."

Since we celebrate Washington's birthday on February 22, one wonders why the record says "11th day of February." The reason is that the English calendar was changed in 1751 to agree with the calendar then in use in most countries of Europe. As a result, the 11th of February became the 22nd, and this date is now observed as the birthday of a great American who ranks among the famous men of world history.

Before he celebrated his sixteenth birthday, young George Washington had already made trips as a surveyor into the frontier counties of Virginia. There were only a few narrow mud roads in the colonies. Beyond the cities along the Atlantic coast, all was wilderness. To wander into the mountains was an adventure only for the brave.

Washington's work as a surveyor gave him knowledge of the backwoods and he learned the meaning of hardship. After he was named as a county surveyor in 1749, he was called upon to travel far and wide over wilderness trails on horseback. Sometimes he rode forty miles a day, and he became one of the best horsemen in the colonies.

Little did Washington realize, in 1754, that one day he would command the armies of a new nation. In that year, at the age of twenty-two, his military career was just beginning. He was made a lieutenant colonel, and was ordered to lead two hundred men to an unfinished fort at a point on the frontier where the Allegheny and Monongahela rivers meet.

Washington's soldiers on that journey were poorly equipped. They complained because they needed blankets and food, but they marched on until they met the French at Great Meadows. In the fight which followed, Washington was successful, and there was quiet for a week or two. It was known, however, that larger forces of the enemy were in the neighborhood. Suddenly, on the fourth day of July, 1754, the French and Indians defeated Washington's forces at Fort Necessity. Three months later he resigned his commission.

In the spring of the next year, Washington enlisted in an army led by Braddock, a British general. Braddock had been sent from England to make a great effort to crush the French forces which had taken strong positions at frontier points of the American colonies.

As the troops advanced toward the western part of Pennsylvania, Washington fell ill with a fever, but he did not give in. Braddock's men were surprised by the French and Indians near Fort Duquesne, and it was the courage of Washington, ill as he was, that kept the men in order when they had to retreat. In reporting the affair in a letter to his mother, Washington wrote that "The Virginia troops showed a good deal of bravery, and were nearly all killed. I luckily escaped without a wound, though I had four bullets through my coat and two horses were shot under me. Two of the aides-de-camp were wounded early in the engagement, which rendered the duty harder upon me, as I was the only person then left to distribute the general's orders, which I was scarcely able to do, as I was not half recovered from a violent illness, that had confined me to bed and a wagon for about ten days." Cool and fearless, Washington was, indeed, the hero of this battle.

The fever, that had made Washington ill, returned with greater force after the battle. For a time the young officer feared that he was going to die, but he was able to work his way back to Mount Vernon in February of 1758. Then he returned to his life as a farmer and country gentleman.

For some years Washington interested himself in the crops on his large farms. When the dispute between England and the American colonies was growing serious, however, Washington met with important men to talk things over. He went to Philadelphia in 1773, and next year attended the sessions of the First Continental Congress in that city.

In 1775 Washington returned once more to Philadelphia. On June 15, two months after the British soldiers and the New England farmers had fought at Lexington and Concord, he was chosen Commander in Chief of the Army of the revolting colonies.

Standing six feet two inches tall, Washington made a deep impression on the delegates when he appeared for the first time in the uniform of the new army. It was blue, trimmed with light tan, with yellow metal buttons, light tan waistcoat and breeches, and white stockings.

Washington's journeys through the country, first as a surveyor and then as an officer, had taught him a great deal. This knowledge proved of high value when he led the colonies in the struggle for independence.

Washington showed his skill on many battlefields, even though he was not the equal in many ways of such a general as Napoleon. Napoleon fought his wars largely to add to his own glory. Washington, on the other hand, loved peace and had no wish to win personal glory at the cost of bloodshed. He led the American Armies simply because he felt that it was his duty to his fellow countrymen.

Washington seemed to bear a charmed life on the battlefield. There is no record that he ever was wounded in the slightest way. The "charm" upon the general's life was, no doubt, only good fortune. Many other Americans in the Revolutionary War also went through the battles without a scratch.

Sometimes we see pictures of Washington standing in the midst of the fighting on the battlefield, an easy target for enemy bullets. Those pictures cannot be considered true to life. The general was in the heat of the fighting from time to time, but he did not go out of his way to run into the path of bullets or cannon balls!

At Valley Forge, American soldiers showed their trust in George Washington and proved how willing they were to suffer for freedom. Valley Forge was a village in the hills twenty miles from Philadelphia. Close to 11,000 soldiers marched there to camp during the winter of 1777-1778. Most of them lived in small, cold huts, which were built hastily. Washington stayed with them at Valley Forge and, when everything seemed darkest, he did much to give them courage to face their troubles.

Time and again the troops heard the news, "No meat today!" Frequently the soldiers felt the pains of hunger. They suffered from the freezing cold because they did not have enough clothing. Some had to walk barefoot over the frozen ground. Washington said that the march of his men might be traced by bloodstains left by their bare, bleeding feet. He begged Congress to send food, shirts, coats, soap and medicine but few of these things ever reached the camp. Under the same hardships the soldiers of some armies might have broken camp and gone home, but the Americans were struggling for a great cause. Neither cold nor hunger could make them yield. They admired their great general whose friendly chats with them lifted their spirits.

During the same winter, thousands of British troops were living comfortably in Philadelphia. Warm, well-fed and well-clothed, they waited for the fighting to begin again in the spring and summer of 1778. When that time came, the ragged men of Valley Forge were to prove more than a match for them.

In one battle Washington showed how it is possible to turn defeat into victory. This was done at the Battle of Monmouth when the tide was going against the Americans.

Through an error of judgment, General Charles Lee had ordered the soldiers to retreat. Suddenly, Washington came riding to the scene, and was told about the order to retreat. Quickly he shouted out the order, "Turn back!" The troops obeyed the Commander in Chief and, when the battle was over, the Americans held the field.

Other battles were to be fought before victory was won by the Americans. The last important battle in the War for Independence resulted in the capture of Yorktown, in Virginia, and the surrender of the British troops under Lord

Cornwallis in October, 1781. A peace treaty with Great Britain was signed in 1783, and the British agreed that the thirteen colonies were free and independent. The land between the Atlantic coast and the Mississippi River, south of Canada, was to belong to the new nation, the United States of America.

With the close of the war, George Washington returned to his home in Virginia to enjoy a well-earned rest. Six years later, however, he was called back to serve his country. He was elected President of the United States, the first man to be chosen under the new constitution. Bidding good-bye to his beautiful estate at Mount Vernon, he mounted a horse and rode northward toward New York, which was then the capital. Along the way he was wildly cheered by crowds which gathered in the villages and towns on his way. Guns were fired and bells were rung, and women and children strewed flowers in his path.

Washington began his term as President on April 30, 1789. John Adams was vice-president, and Thomas Jefferson was secretary of state.

At the end of four years, Washington was again elected President. The new country was already growing. Three new states were added to the union. They were Vermont, Kentucky and Tennessee. Kentucky had belonged to Virginia, and Tennessee had been part of North Carolina.

After finishing his second term, Washington decided to return to his plantations. He journeyed back to Mount Vernon, where he spent most of his time during the last years of his life. He died on December 12, 1799, at the age of sixty-seven.

One of the generals who had served under him in the War for Independence was Henry Lee, a fellow Virginian, nicknamed "Light-Horse Harry." He paid Washington a tribute which has lasted down through time. He spoke of Washington as:

"First in war, first in peace, and first in the hearts of his countrymen."

JOHN PAUL JONES

JOHN PAUL JONES

Master of the Bonhomme Richard

BORN 1747—DIED 1792

I HAVE NOT YET begun to fight!"

Those words were spoken by John Paul Jones in 1779, and they have echoed down the years. They were addressed to a British naval captain who had asked whether an American warship was ready to strike its colors in surrender.

Jones was born in Scotland, and was the son of a gardener. Strangely enough, his family name was Paul, not Jones. He adopted the name of Jones in his young manhood, as a mark of respect to a North Carolina man, Willie Jones, who had proved a good friend to him after he came to live in the American colonies.

As a twelve-year-old boy, he went to sea aboard a British merchant ship. In the years which followed he made several voyages to the American coast, where he saw an older brother who had settled in Virginia. By the time he was twenty-one, he had reached the rank of mate on a British vessel carrying on trade with Africa.

The death of his older brother brought a change in his life, because his brother's property was left to him. Giving up the sea, he settled in Virginia in 1773.

Only two years later, the War for American Independence broke out, and John Paul Jones was quick to take the side of his adopted country. He offered his services to fight in the newly formed Navy, and shortly was made lieutenant aboard the *Alfred*, flagship of a small American fleet. He is said to have been the first man to raise the Stars and Stripes on an American warship.

Aboard the *Alfred*, Jones sailed to the West Indies, and played a part in a successful raid against a British fort on one of the islands. Soon afterward he was given command of the sloop *Providence*, and helped convoy some of General Washington's troops from Rhode Island to New York City.

In the summer of 1776 Jones sailed his sloop into the Atlantic Ocean, watching for British ships bound for Nova Scotia and the Gulf of St. Lawrence. One by one he captured sixteen British merchant ships. Eight of them he brought safely to Newport harbor in Rhode Island, having destroyed the rest because he did not have enough sailors to man them.

Jones' next adventure took him across the Atlantic, aboard a small warship, the *Ranger*. He did not expect to do much with a vessel of such size, but he had been promised command of a fine frigate which was being built in Holland.

After reaching Europe, Jones met with disappointment. He was told that the owners of the frigate had sold it to France, fearing that otherwise it would be seized by the British.

There was a spirit in John Paul Jones which could not be held down. With his small *Ranger* he now dared to raid the British coast! Sailing into Solway Firth in the dead of night, he landed at the head of a band of daring men. They slipped into a fort which guarded the harbor of Whitehaven. The sentinels were asleep in a nearby guardhouse, and Jones was able to spike the guns of the fort so that they could not be used against him. Having finished this task, the Americans made their way to another fort and treated it the same way. A little later, with his own hands, Jones set fire to a British sailing vessel. He hoped that the flames would spread to the other merchant ships in the harbor, but this did not happen, since the crews took them out of the way of danger. News of the raid spread throughout Great Britain, and caused alarm lest the bold American captain might attack other points.

Jones appeared next off the coast of Ireland, and fought against the *Drake*, a small British warship. The fight lasted an hour and four minutes before the *Drake* surrendered.

Jones then sailed to France, where Benjamin Franklin had been busy for months trying to bring the French into the war on the American side. Franklin talked with the captain, and promised to do what he could to supply him with a larger warship. At last a vessel called the *Duras* was turned over to him.

The *Duras* was an old merchant ship. Some of her timbers were half-rotted and her speed was slow, even for a sailing vessel. Jones gave her a new name, the *Bonhomme Richard,* in honor of Franklin, the author of "Poor Richard's Almanack." It took months to turn this vessel into a warship. Then the captain had to accept several cannon which the French Government did not consider fit for use in war. A crew of 380 men was gathered, of whom only about eighty were Americans. The rest were chiefly French, Portuguese and Swedes.

With France now turning to active war against Great Britain, Jones was able to gather a few small ships to sail along with the *Bonhomme Richard,* but at best they did not amount to a great deal. What a tiny fleet it was to dare the navy of Great Britain, the Mistress of the Seas!

To Jones, however, all things were possible. On a September day in 1779 he spotted forty-one British ships in the North Sea, sailing toward the British coast, which was not far distant. For the most part they were merchant ships with no cannon aboard, but a frigate and a sloop of war were on guard.

Giving over the task of attacking the sloop to the other vessels in his fleet, Jones steered his own ship toward the frigate, which carried the name of *Serapis.* The two vessels came within hailing distance in the twilight. When it was plain to both that they were enemies of each other, broadsides were exchanged.

Two of the old cannon on the *Bonhomme Richard* burst when the first broadside was fired. The men handling them were killed, and a big hole was torn in the side of the ship. The *Serapis* had fifty guns against the forty now left on the American vessel.

Captain Pearson, of the *Serapis,* found that his warship could move faster than the American ship. Therefore he sailed around to the stern, into which he could send a raking broadside. These shots had a telling effect, but in the growing darkness the British ship passed too close. Seeing the bowsprit of the *Serapis* hanging over the deck of his own ship, Jones called for a hawser. Very speedily he lashed the bowsprit to one of his own masts. The bowsprit of the *Serapis* broke off, but the rigging of the two ships had become so closely tangled that they could not at once be separated. Sails had been shot down by both sides. There was great excitement. At length two of the men on the American ship suddenly called out that it was sinking. Jones heard them, and threw two pistols at them, knocking one senseless, and calling them both scoundrels for shouting out such a report.

It was at this ticklish moment that the British captain asked the question which brought the unforgettable reply, "I have not yet begun to fight!" From that day to this, Americans have remembered these fighting words of John Paul Jones.

The *Bonhomme Richard* was not actually sinking, but she was leaking, and the pumps had to be used to keep her afloat. The men on both ships kept firing their cannon, and much wreckage littered the decks. The ships were now fighting side by side in the moonlight. A British boarding party tried to get on the *Bonhomme Richard*, but American sharpshooters drove them back with heavy loss.

Something strange now happened. One of the ships, which had sailed with Jones, came within gun range. It might have given welcome help, but it was under command of a Frenchman who later was judged to be ill-balanced in mind. Ordered to action, his gunners fired volleys of grapeshot which caused as much damage to the Americans as to the British. The British captain, however, did not know that the Americans were suffering in equal measure. He saw a second American warship coming near, and, fearing another rain of shot, decided it would be best to surrender.

Both vessels were afire when the *Serapis* struck her colors. The sailors soon were able to quench the flames, but many hours were needed to clear the wreckage from the decks.

The next day Jones inspected the two ships, and saw that the *Serapis* was in better condition than his *Bonhomme Richard*. It was a much newer vessel, and had been better able to stand the pounding. His own ship was in fact slowly sinking, and sadly the captain was forced to order his men to abandon their vessel and transfer to the captured ship. On the second day after the fight, the *Bonhomme Richard* went to the bottom.

Shortly after winning the fight against the *Serapis,* Captain Jones learned that one of the vessels of his little fleet had captured the British sloop of war, although the merchant ships under escort had escaped in the night. The action, all in all, was an important victory.

John Paul Jones lived for some years after the close of the War for American Independence in which he had served so bravely. He was awarded a gold medal by the Congress of the United States for his daring as commander of the *Bonhomme Richard.* The closing years of his life he spent in Europe, chiefly in Russia and France. Falling victim to an illness, he died in Paris in 1792 when he was only forty-five years of age.

LORD NELSON

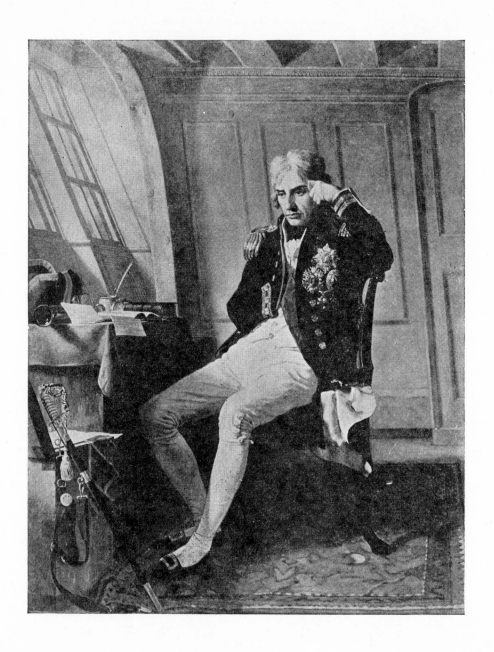

LORD NELSON

England's Greatest Admiral

BORN 1758—DIED 1805

I<small>N THE SUMMER</small> of 1770 there lived in the English county of Norfolk a minister with eight children. The mother of the children had died, and the father was worried as to how to take care of so many children.

The worries of that family might have had little place in history if the father had not decided to take the course he did for one of his sons. The son was Horatio Nelson, and he was not quite twelve years old. In September, 1770, Horatio was sent to London where he was under the care of his mother's brother. This uncle was a captain in the royal navy.

Horatio traveled by stagecoach to London over the bumpy roads of those days, but the lad was to meet far rougher journeys in the life that was ahead. Shortly after his twelfth birthday a place was found for him aboard a vessel bound for the New World. The youth's work at sea was at first that of cabin boy, and he followed it for three years. After returning from the West Indies, he went on another voyage, this time to the north Atlantic, beyond the Arctic Circle.

Nelson's third long voyage was made when he was fifteen years old. This time he went around the southern tip of Africa and across the Indian Ocean to Sumatra and Java in the East Indies. During part of the trip he was rated as an able seaman, but by the end of the voyage he had become a midshipman.

Although young Nelson was destined to be a famous admiral, it seemed, when he was only seventeen, that his days on the sea might be at an end. During his stay in the Orient, he fell sick and lost the use of his limbs. When the vessel which brought him home docked in England, he was put ashore as an invalid. The good care which he received after landing helped to bring him back to health. He regained the use of his limbs, and in a few months took an examination for an officer's rank in the Navy. After passing the examination he was made a lieutenant.

In his new rank Nelson crossed the Atlantic to Jamaica. This trip was made during the time of the War for American Independence. Nelson, however, saw little action in the war, but took part in the convoy of vessels carrying cargo.

Captains of naval vessels in these days usually are men of middle age, seldom being under the age of forty. In Nelson's day, however, young men sometimes rose quickly to high rank. When he was only twenty years of age, he was made a captain.

Although he rose in rank, Nelson still suffered from poor health. After going to Central America, he was struck down by fever, and was not expected to recover. Fortunately, he got back enough strength to permit him to return once more to England. There he fought the illness, and became well enough to sail to Canada. Later he wrote that he really won back his health in "Fair Canada."

When the War for American Independence was a thing of the past, Nelson visited France and studied the French language. He also studied French methods of sea warfare. The visit to France was to prove of value after the rise of Napoleon Bonaparte. When Great Britain later went to war against the French, every fact Nelson knew about French methods of warfare turned out to be useful and important.

The war with France broke out in 1793, and it found Nelson captain of of the *Agamemnon*. He went into active service and directed the fighting against several French men-of-war. His skill was so great that he soon rose to the rank of rear admiral. As a young rear admiral he was in command of the British fleet at the famous Battle of the Nile on August 1, 1798. Napoleon at that time hoped to win mastery over Egypt, and for that purpose had sent a powerful fleet to an Egyptian port.

Even with a smaller fleet, Nelson was anxious to attack, and well did he plan the battle. Finding the French at anchor, he sailed toward them and fought them one or two at a time. The French could not sail against the wind, so the farther vessels were unable to come to the rescue of those which were under fire. The outcome was an important British victory.

Some persons blame lack of success in what they want to do upon ill health, but many men and women have proved that this is not always a good excuse. In spite of sickness, they have won the objects which they have set out to reach. Horatio Nelson never was very strong in body. From boyhood onward he suffered from one illness after another, yet he led Great Britain to some of the greatest naval victories in her history.

From the time he first became a captain, Nelson was a good friend of the men under his command. He did all he could for their comfort, and made sure they were paid proper wages. As a result, the sailors grew very fond of him. After he became a rear admiral, he was always thoughtful and kindly in his dealings with the captains in his fleet as well as with the sailors. The captains, in their turn, were most loyal to him at all times, and were ready to follow him through any battle, no matter how greatly the odds seemed against success.

During one of his battles Nelson lost his right arm, and in another he was blinded in one eye. Both times he displayed high courage. After the Battle of the Nile he was hailed as one of Britain's great heroes, and was given the title of "Baron Nelson of the Nile." He also was voted a yearly pension amounting to $10,000 in our money. The rulers of Russia and Turkey sent him rich presents. They, too, were pleased that a heavy blow had been dealt against Napoleon.

Napoleon, however, was far from being knocked out of the war. Some of his most important victories on land were ahead of him. Even on the sea, he was to grow dangerous again. There were short periods of peace, and Nelson used them to go back to England where he could rest and build up his health. One vacation was broken when he was sent to Denmark in the spring of 1801 to take part in the Battle of Copenhagen. He was second in command on the British side. At one point in the battle, Admiral Parker gave him a signal to withdraw, but Nelson, in telling later about his own action, said that he put his blind eye to the telescope and could not see the signal! By stubborn fighting, under the direction of Nelson, the British were able to turn the tide and defeat the enemy.

The year 1805 saw the most important of all Nelson's battles. It is known as the Battle of Trafalgar. Cape Trafalgar is south of the city of Cadiz, Spain, and is near the Atlantic entrance to the Strait of Gibraltar. Nelson was in command of the fleet of twenty-seven British warships which sailed to attack a larger French and Spanish fleet. Spain at that time was under Napoleon's power and was classed as an ally of France.

Thirty-three vessels with 2,640 cannon were ranged against Nelson. The British had only 2,138 cannon, but they had the service of a skillful leader. He planned the battle in such a way that the enemy fleet could be cut in two. Before the actual fighting started on that October day, Admiral Nelson issued his famous message. Sailors and officers of the entire fleet were told, "England expects every man to do his duty."

Aboard the *Victory*, the admiral pressed into the thick of the conflict. In three hours the main part of the fighting was over. Fifteen French or Spanish vessels were sunk that afternoon, and two weeks later the British were to capture four of those which had escaped. On the British side, not a single warship was lost!

So ended the famous Battle of Trafalgar, but in the midst of it Admiral Nelson had fallen to the deck mortally wounded. He was carried below, but his men knew he could not live. Before he died he was given the happy news of the British victory. "I have done my duty," breathed Nelson as he lay dying.

Horatio Nelson, usually spoken of as Lord Nelson, was forty-seven years old at the time of his death. His success at sea had done a great deal to wear down the power of Napoleon. He has been called "the greatest admiral in history" and surely ranks among the best of the world's naval leaders.

ANDREW JACKSON

ANDREW JACKSON

Old Hickory

BORN 1767—DIED 1845

A NDREW JACKSON might well be called "the orphan boy who became president." His father died a few days before Andrew was born, and when he was fourteen years old, his mother passed away.

Andrew's parents had very little money and few possessions, but within the boy there was a spirit that made him stand out among his fellows. He was hot-tempered and proud, and it was said of him that he would "fight at the drop of a hat." This forceful spirit remained with him after he reached manhood, and led him to fight duels, and do other things which a man with better self-control would not have done.

The question is still unsettled as to whether Andrew Jackson was born in North Carolina or South Carolina. It seems that the place of his birth was on a plantation close to the borderline of those two colonies at a time when careful surveys had not been made. He, himself, later stated that he was born near Waxhaw Creek, South Carolina, on March 15, 1767. The father, whom he never knew, was a farm laborer who only two years before had left northern Ireland with his family to settle in the New World. His name, too, was Andrew Jackson.

Mrs. James Crawford, sister of Mrs. Jackson, welcomed the infant Andrew, his two older brothers and their mother in her home on a nearby plantation. The sister, an invalid, was glad to have help in managing the eight children in her own family.

As it turned out, however, the eleven boys and girls in the Crawford household from that time onward were not too well managed. Indeed, they often ran wild, and Andrew became perhaps the wildest of the lot. He was rough and ready, eager for all sports and especially fond of cock-fighting during his boyhood.

With only a little schooling now and then, Andrew reached the age of thirteen. Then, in company with Robert, his sixteen-year-old brother, he joined a company of soldiers fighting on the American side in the War for American Independence. The commander put him on duty as a mounted messenger, and gave him a pistol. A tall, thin, blue-eyed boy with reddish-brown hair, he did what he could for the cause of freedom. Knowing horses well, he proved to be an excellent rider on the roads and trails of the district. He was as prompt and careful as he could be about following orders.

Yet his service in the Revolution was short-lived. He was captured by the British after an exciting chase, and was set free only when his mother came to the enemy camp and begged for his release. While a prisoner, he was ordered to blacken the boots of an officer. He refused, and the angry officer struck him with his sword. The wound left a scar on his head which showed plainly all his life.

Mrs. Jackson was allowed by the British to help nurse the American prisoners, many of whom had smallpox. In this service, she herself fell sick and died. The war also cost the lives of the two elder boys, leaving Andrew without brothers as well as without parents.

With the fighting over, the youth tried in one way after another to find a trade. For a few weeks he worked at making saddles for horses, but decided that this was not what he wanted to do. He even attempted to teach school, despite the fact that he had had only scraps of education himself.

At the age of seventeen, Andrew Jackson began to study law under the direction of a well-known attorney in Salisbury, North Carolina. Just how he paid his living expenses at that time, we are not told, but he kept at the law long enough to become a lawyer.

At the age of twenty-one, the young lawyer made his way to Nashville, a frontier settlement in what was to be the state of Tennessee. There he was made public prosecutor, and rose swiftly in politics. Shortly after Tennessee became a state, he was chosen by its people as a member of the Congress at Washington. A year later he became United States Senator, but served only a year in this office before giving it up to accept a place as supreme court judge in Tennessee. For six years he stayed on the supreme court, and then resigned.

When the War of 1812 broke out, Andrew Jackson was ready to take an active part in the fighting. As a major general of the state militia, he took command of 2,500 men, marching them to Natchez, a point on the Mississippi River, now in the state of Mississippi. Orders came from Washington, however, for him to disband his men at once. His soldiers were mostly boys; many of them were wounded. He could not turn them loose so far from home, so he himself arranged to supply them with food and led them back to Tennessee.

It was at this time that the nickname of "Old Hickory" seems to have been used for the first time. The soldiers said that their leader was "as tough as hickory," and from this sprang the nickname by which Jackson was known the rest of his life.

In 1813 Jackson was badly wounded in the shoulder during a quarrel which arose from a misunderstanding regarding a duel in which a friend was to take part. Before this, in a duel he himself had fought, he had had a rib broken, but his present wound was the most serious he had suffered. Before it was healed, and with his arm still in a sling, Jackson fought in a campaign against the Creek Indians in Alabama. These Indians were among the many tribesmen who made attacks on American settlements during the War of 1812.

Now, for the first time, Jackson was able to show his quick wit and skill in battle. After winning several skirmishes, he closed in on the Creeks at Horseshoe Bend, on the banks of a river which flows through eastern Alabama. The Indians were badly defeated.

The Battle of Horseshoe Bend took place on March 27, 1814. Shortly afterward, Jackson became a major general in the regular Army of the United States. He made a quick capture of Pensacola, in northern Florida, which the British had been using even though the territory was, at that time,

Spanish soil. After the arrival of the Americans, the British fleet sailed out of the harbor of Pensacola.

Marching westward, Jackson and his men next prepared to defend New Orleans from British attack. Feeling certain that the attack would come from the south, the general made ready a line four miles below the city. This line stretched from a swamp to the eastern bank of the Mississippi River. Trenches were dug, and breastworks were built, partly of cotton bales. Defending that line and an area west of the river were 5,500 American soldiers. Twelve thousand troops were laying siege to New Orleans. On January 8, 1815, a large part of the British Army, under cover of a fog, marched to attack the line set up by Jackson. More than 2,000 British soldiers were killed, but the Americans suffered only about seventy casualties.

News of the victory spread slowly through the United States. There were no telegraph lines to carry word of what had happened. People in New York and New England did not learn about it for weeks. At about the same time they heard about the Battle of New Orleans, they received news of another kind from across the Atlantic Ocean. At Ghent, Belgium, a treaty of peace had been signed by Great Britain and the United States on December 24, 1814—fifteen days before the battle had been fought!

If there had been a cable across the Atlantic and a telegraph line from the Atlantic seaboard to New Orleans, there would have been no Battle of New Orleans, and the lives of many soldiers would have been saved. As it was, Jackson won the only important land battle on the American side in the entire war. His name and fame spread over the land, and after the passing of some years, "Old Hickory" was elected President of the United States.

Andrew Jackson served two terms as president, having been elected in 1828 and 1832. His years in office were filled with incidents which showed his fiery nature. At one time the state of South Carolina tried to defy the tariff laws of the national government. Jackson, himself, did not believe that the tariff laws were good, but he declared that, as long as they had been passed, they must be obeyed. To South Carolina's threat to leave the Union, he replied by sending warships and soldiers to the Charleston area, saying, "The Federal Union—it must and shall be obeyed!" Partly by the prompt action of the

President, and partly by the action of Congress in changing the laws, the South Carolina trouble was ended.

In his seventy-eighth year, Andrew Jackson died at "The Hermitage," his home near Nashville. Along with Thomas Jefferson, he is looked upon as one of the founders of the Democratic Party.

WELLINGTON

WELLINGTON

The Iron Duke

BORN 1769—DIED 1852

It MAY SEEM STRANGE that a bad attack of fever could do a man a good turn, but that is just what happened in the case of a young colonel in the British Army.

The colonel was in India at the time—the year 1801—and had been ordered to sail to Egypt. Having made ready with his soldiers, he was about to board the transport *Susanna* when he fell ill. Another officer took his place, and he was left behind.

Out in the Indian Ocean, the *Susanna* was lost, with all on board. It was a fearful tragedy, and, when the colonel learned of it, he must have wondered about the twist of fate which had saved him from the doom of the man who had taken his place.

The officer who escaped disaster was Arthur Wellesley, and he was thirty-two years old at the time. As he lay on his sick bed, little did he know that he was to become famous at a future day, and was to be honored with the title of "Duke of Wellington."

Having recovered from his illness, Wellesley once more took up his military work in India. Two years later he was in command of 9,500 troops, half of them natives, and was facing an Indian rajah who had risen in rebellion. The situation was serious.

The rajah's army was far larger than Wellesley's, being composed of close to 40,000 well-drilled foot soldiers and trained cavalrymen. Both sides had scores of cannon. The fight which occurred is known as the Battle of

Assaye. By a bold stroke, Wellesley defeated the enemy and put the rajah's army to flight. More victories followed in the next three months, and finally a treaty was made, bringing the rebellion to an end.

Following this success, Wellesley went back to the British Isles. Soon after he landed, he was elected to the House of Parliament. Although he had been born in Ireland, he was a member of an old English family, and was the fourth son of an earl.

As a boy Wellesley had gone to Eton, and later had studied at a military school in France. At neither place had he shown himself a good scholar and, indeed, there were some who had described him as "a dunce." In the military field, however, he was to rise step by step.

Across the English Channel there was a man of the same age, who had made far greater progress in the art of war. This man was Napoleon Bonaparte. Like Wellesley, he was thirty-six years old, but Napoleon was already known all over Europe as a general and a ruler. He had led his armies against nation after nation on the continent of Europe, and had won many important victories.

Shortly before Wellesley landed in England after his return from India, Napoleon was laying plans for an invasion of Great Britain. Had those plans been carried out, Wellesley probably would have served in the forces fighting off the invasion, but he would not have been commander-in-chief. He had won his spurs in India, but he had not yet fought the battles which were to bring him the rank of general.

Only on the sea had the forces of Napoleon suffered any real defeat up to this time. Lord Nelson, British admiral, had won the Battle of the Nile, and in 1805 he was to defeat Napolean's fleet in the Battle of Trafalgar.

Shortly before he left for Trafalgar, Nelson met young Colonel Wellesley while waiting in the ante-room of the Colonial Office in London. Nelson probably knew something about the colonel's recent victories in India, but he never was to know that the man with whom he spoke would finally whip Napoleon at Waterloo. Only a month later the great admiral's death was to take place off Cape Trafalgar.

Three years after the Battle of Trafalgar, Wellesley sailed to Portugal. By

80

this time he had been promoted to the rank of lieutenant general, and he was to be in command of a long campaign against Napoleon.

It proved a fairly simple matter for the British Army to drive the French out of Portugal in 1808, but the fighting in Spain was far harder. It dragged on year after year. The British under command of Wellesley won several victories, but the soldiers of Napoleon were able to keep much Spanish territory in their hands.

Napoleon, himself, was not in direct command of the French troops in Spain. He was busy both in Paris and on certain battlefronts where he took personal charge of his armies. It was in 1812 that he made his greatest mistake. At the head of an army of great size, he invaded Russia. The Russian winter, with its biting cold, and the Russian Army defeated him, driving him out with only a few pitiful remnants of his large invasion forces. Thus the French power suffered damage from which real recovery never came.

Meanwhile the British had been making slow but sure progress in Spain. If Napoleon had gathered a new army and had marched into Spain, he might have halted the British advance.

As it was, Napoleon did raise a new army, but he had to use it to fight in central Europe. Prussia and Sweden had joined Russia in that area, and they seemed to offer the strongest threat to his power. Those three countries, along with Great Britain, were called "the Allies." They were defeated in battles with the French at Bautzen and Dresden, but in the autumn of 1813 they won a great victory at Leipzig, in what has since been called the "Battle of the Nations."

After the defeat at Leipzig, Napoleon saw that the end was coming. Furthermore, news of other victories by the British was brought to him, and he could see that he was about to be crushed from both sides.

The British were still under the command of Wellesley, now known as Viscount Wellington. The new title had been given him because of his success in Spain, and for the rest of his life he was almost always known as "Wellington."

Early in 1814 Wellington found himself in southern France, pressing on toward Paris. Before he reached the French capital, Napoleon had been

81

forced to give up the throne, and had been sent as a prisoner to the island of Elba in the Mediterranean Sea.

For the important part he played in the downfall of Napoleon, Wellington was given even higher honors. He was raised to the rank of field marshal and was made Duke of Wellington.

It looked as if Europe would be free of worries over Napoleon, but in ten months the Little Corporal was back. He had escaped from Elba. Quickly raising an army in southern France, he reached Paris in triumph and was hailed once more as the ruler of France.

The former allies again gathered their strength as fast as possible, and made ready to meet Napoleon on the continent of Europe. Wellington was at the head of the united armies.

At a little-known village in Belgium the two armies faced each other to fight one of the most famous battles in history, the Battle of Waterloo. In a field near the village, on June 18, 1815, Wellington's army met Napoleon's. During most of the fighting, Napoleon had the advantage of a slightly larger force, but in the evening many thousands of troops led by von Blücher, a Prussian general, arrived to reinforce Wellington's armies and the French were soon put to flight. This battle decided the fate of Napoleon.

Shortly after the Battle of Waterloo, Napoleon was captured and sent to St. Helena, an island far down in the South Atlantic. From this remote island the prisoner could not escape!

As the foremost general in the struggle against Napoleon, the Duke of Wellington earned lasting fame. He returned to England and before many years passed was made prime minister. He lived to the ripe age of eighty-two. Because of the strength and firmness he showed in war, he was nicknamed "the Iron Duke."

NAPOLEON

NAPOLEON

Master of Europe

BORN 1769—DIED 1821

In the year 1794, a young man was placed under arrest in southern France. He had been trained as an army officer, and had served the new Republic of France in battle. Lately, however, he had been accused of acting against the republic, and that is why he was held prisoner in a fort near the city of Nice.

The young man was Napoleon Bonaparte. If he had been found guilty and held prisoner for many years, the history of Europe would have been different. It seems almost certain that France would not have kept on making war during such a long period. The lives of hundreds of thousands of Frenchmen, Italians, Germans and Englishmen might have been saved.

As it was, the charge against Napoleon was declared false, and he was set free. There were many who thought he would help the newborn republic with the battles ahead.

Napoleon was born on the island of Corsica, not far from the French coast. As a boy he was sent to France to attend a military school, and at the age of only sixteen he became an officer in the French Army. Thus, while still a youth, he showed special skill in military training.

France was a kingdom at that time, but trouble was only a short distance away. Many persons were angry about the way in which the nobles and the king ran the country. They felt that the common people were not being treated justly. This led to revolt. King Louis XVI and his queen were made prisoners, and were put to death. A large number of nobles also suffered the same fate during the years of the French Revolution, a period of great and important change.

While France was having these troubles, Napoleon went back to Corsica. He wanted Corsica to become free from France, and he also wanted power for himself.

Having met with little success in Corsica, however, he left the island and sailed once more to France. Soon he helped to direct a successful attack on the port of Toulon, which was in the hands of the British. The British were forced to leave the city.

The victory did not bring quick personal triumph for the little Corsican. Soon afterward he was under arrest, but was held only a short time in the prison fort near Nice before being freed. Then he went to Paris.

In Paris there were thousands who wanted to bring back the old line of kings. They hoped to place a prince of the Bourbon family on the throne. Napoleon was chosen to help lead the fight against this party. He ordered cannon to be loaded with grapeshot and fired into the midst of people who were against the republic.

Some persons in the Paris gatherings were cut down by the grapeshot which Napoleon's cannoneers fired into them. The attempt to overthrow the new republic had failed, and the plan of bringing back the old line of kings was ended for a long while.

Young Napoleon became the man of the hour, and was chosen to command a French Army in northern Italy. Although Italian blood flowed in his veins, he was willing to fight against the men of Italy.

Napoleon was only five feet and two inches tall. Nature had made him a little man, but he firmly believed that he could make himself a great man. His mind was keen, and he knew how to handle soldiers. After taking command as general, he sent this message to the army: "I will take you to the most fertile plains in the world. Rich provinces and great cities will be in your power. You will find honor, glory and wealth."

Italy at that time was not the united country it later became. Much of the northern part was under the power of Austria. Napoleon's army fought

86

against soldiers from the island of Sardinia, from provinces of Italy, and from Austria.

Time and again, the French were victors. There was power in the little general, power to see the best way to win battles. At one time he risked his own life by going to the front line of the battle and out upon a bridge which he had ordered his army to cross. The crossing was made under very heavy fire from the Austrian batteries. Once more, Napoleon was the winner.

Soon afterward he marched into the city of Milan, feeling as proud as a conqueror of olden days. In the months which followed, he crossed northern Italy and made himself master of Venice. He was able to boast that he had obtained and sent to Paris exquisite works of art, some of them hundreds of years old. Much of this booty was returned to Italy after his downfall.

At length, peace was made, and the general, now twenty-eight years of age, returned to Paris. Although he was hailed as a hero, he was not content. In his mind there grew strong the idea of making himself master of Egypt. The men at the head of the French Republic were glad, indeed, to have him leave for a war in such a distant land. They had called on him for help as a general, but now they feared that he might try to make himself ruler of France.

On a spring day in the year 1798, Bonaparte set sail with an army of 38,000 men, aboard hundreds of vessels. He was on his way to Egypt.

Egypt, at that time, was part of the Turkish Empire, and Napoleon wanted to take it from the Turks. By doing so, he believed he would give French merchants a hold on the trade route to India.

Because British merchants had most of India's trade, Napoleon knew that Great Britain might stand in the way of his conquest of Egypt. He was ready to fight the British, but did not want the fighting to take place on the sea. The Navy of Great Britain was stronger than that of France.

When he reached Egypt, Napoleon and his soldiers fought against native troops and defeated them. He gained control of Alexandria, Cairo and other parts of northern Egypt.

After a time, however, Lord Nelson's British fleet sailed to Egypt and fought against Napoleon's war vessels in a battle near the delta of the Nile. The

87

French lost the Battle of the Nile, and Napoleon was left with a puzzling problem. He was master of Egypt, but he had no way of sailing back to Europe with his army. The British fleet would block the way.

Deciding to leave his army in Egypt, Napoleon made a secret trip back to France. He arrived after weeks of slow sailing in a small boat and had several narrow escapes from the British.

On his return to Paris, Napoleon entered into a plot to change the control of the French Government. The plot was carried out successfully, and Napoleon obtained political power. He called himself the "First Consul of the Republic." For a time, there were two other consuls, but they had little power compared with that of Napoleon.

The French Army which had been left in Egypt gave up after a time, and was allowed to return to France. Except for the fact that some thousands of men, mostly Egyptians and Turks, had been killed, the conquest of Egypt had amounted to nothing.

When Napoleon took office as consul, he promised that he would guard the republic. A few years later, in 1804, he broke that promise, and had himself declared emperor. He was then only thirty-five years old.

After putting on royal robes of an old pattern, he entered the cathedral of Notre Dame at Paris. Among those present was the Pope. It had been arranged that the Pope should place on the general's head a crown of golden laurel leaves, but to the surprise of all, Napoleon picked up the crown and placed it on his own head! This was one more strange action of a strange man.

Eight years after he made himself supreme ruler of the French, Napoleon led an army into Russia, the empire of Czar Alexander. Five hundred thousand men gathered under the banner of the Emperor Napoleon, who had not yet reached the age of forty-two. Off they marched to war, off to win glory, as they hoped. Not all the soldiers went of their own free will. Only about half were French. The rest were Poles, Dutchmen, Italians and others who had been forced to come from lands over which Napoleon had won power.

Napoleon's plan was not simply to add to his personal glory. He also wanted to reduce the trade of Great Britain, the country which he thought was France's worst enemy. Years before, he had asked the Czar of Russia to shut off Russian trade with the British. This had been done for a time, but then Czar Alexander began to open his ports again. The French emperor grew angry. He would force the Russians to obey his will!

So off to war marched the army of Napoleon. Seven hundred miles had to be covered to reach Moscow. The army was large, and it needed an abundant supply of food. Within a few weeks the soldiers found that there was not enough bread for all. Some fell by the wayside, unable to walk farther. There were deaths from hunger and deaths from disease.

The Russian soldiers kept retreating. Their leaders did not want a general battle. Villages, even cities, were burned by the Russians during their retreat. This left a wasted country through which Napoleon's army had to march.

At last a stand was made by the Russians and a big battle was fought not far from Moscow. Thirty thousand of Napoleon's men and about 40,000 Russians fell. The Russians had to give up the city of Moscow, but they left it ablaze.

Napoleon won Moscow but failed to conquer Russia. Winter was coming on, yet the Czar would not make peace.

Rather than spend a long, cold winter in Russia, Napoleon decided to return to France. His army had shrunk in numbers and supplies were running out.

Hunger and cold weather followed on the heels of Napoleon's men as they trudged painfully back. The emperor felt that he was not traveling fast enough and so, in disguise, he went ahead in a sleigh with a few of his friends. At last he reached France, and much later came a few thousand worn-out, ragged and hungry men, all that had come back of his grand army of half a million soldiers.

Hunger and bad weather explain Napoleon's failure to conquer Russia, but less than a year after his return to France he met actual military defeat on a field of battle.

After gathering a new army of 200,000 men, he marched into Germany and defeated the Austrians at Dresden. Later he was faced by 300,000 Germans, Austrians and others near Leipzig in 1812. This time the Frenchmen lost, and those who were not killed or captured were driven back across the Rhine River.

Next spring the enemies of France were able to reach Paris. Napoleon was forced to surrender his power and was sent into exile on the island of Elba in the Mediterranean. A Bourbon was once again placed on the French throne, and was hailed as King Louis XVIII.

If a better guard had been kept around Napoleon's island home, the people of Europe would have been spared a great deal of bloodshed. As it was, Napoleon escaped. A sailing vessel slipped unnoticed past the British fleet, and aboard it was the little general. He reached France after having been in exile for only ten months.

His old soldiers—those who were still alive—flocked around him and, as he marched into Paris, King Louis promptly left.

Napoleon knew that the other nations of Europe would not willingly accept him as the ruler of France, so he went forth to strike a blow against them and strengthen his own position. On the field of Waterloo, in Belgium, his soldiers charged against the army of British, Germans, Dutch and Belgians. For a time French victory seemed possible, but then came a Prussian army to help Napoleon's enemies.

Down to defeat went the soldiers of the Great Napoleon. It was to be the end of all the general's battles. The Duke of Wellington, British leader of the Allies, was the hero of the day.

Napoleon went back to Paris, but this time not in honor. Many among the leaders of the French wanted to put him out of the way once and for all, so that France could make peace. Fearful of what might happen to himself, he made his way to the coast. He hoped to find a vessel to take him to the United States, but his way was blocked and there was nothing for him to do but go aboard a British ship, the *Bellerophon,* which was waiting in the harbor.

This time he was very closely guarded and sent as a captive to a small rocky island far away in the South Atlantic. The island, St. Helena, was Napoleon's home during the last six years of his life and here the one-time general and emperor had time to think of the way he had spent his life.

STEPHEN DECATUR

STEPHEN DECATUR

The Shores of Tripoli

BORN 1779—DIED 1820

Commandos did not become famous until the second World War, but some wars of the past have seen daring men carry on much the same style of fighting. Soldiers and sailors have made raids on enemy coasts, hurrying away to avoid the aroused enemy.

In naval history no commando-type raid ranks above that of Stephen Decatur in the war against the Barbary pirates. With a small force of men on a small vessel, he entered the harbor where enemy warships lay at anchor, and performed his mission.

Decatur was born in a Maryland village on January 5, 1779, while the American Revolutionary War was being fought. Soon afterward, his parents took him to Philadelphia, where he attended school and spent most of his boyhood.

Stephen's mother wanted him to become a minister in his church, but he was not interested and felt no desire to prepare for that work. Instead, he longed to go to sea, thus following in the footsteps of his father, a sea captain who had commanded a twenty-ton sloop of war in the American Navy.

When only nineteen, young Decatur began to see his wish come true. He was appointed a midshipman aboard the *United States,* a forty-four-gun frigate in the American navy. This ship was to be under his command in an important sea fight some years later.

Soon afterward, Decatur was promoted to the rank of lieutenant. While his ship was in waters off the West Indies, one of the sailors fell overboard.

A small boat was made ready to go to the rescue, but the man might have been drowned if Decatur had not dived into the water and reached his side. He held the sailor above water until the boat reached them. This act of personal heroism was to be followed by a daring feat, under his direction, far away from the shores of America.

The city of Tripoli, in North Africa, on the Mediterranean Sea, was the headquarters of the enemy during warfare against the Barbary pirates. A large frigate, the *Philadelphia*, had been captured by Moorish pirates after running on a reef. Later, the pirates took advantage of high tide to float it again, and sailed it into the harbor of Tripoli.

On the night of February 16, 1804, young Lieutenant Decatur sailed into the harbor. He was in command of a small twelve-gun schooner, with only seventy-five sailors and nine officers aboard.

The Moors aboard the captured *Philadelphia* supposed that a friendly vessel was approaching. In the dim light of the harbor, they could see only six men on the deck. They had all been disguised as Moors. The pilot, a man picked up at the island of Malta, called out to ask for permission to fasten lines to the anchors of the *Philadelphia*. The request was granted, and a line was sent out and fastened before the Moors began to shout "Americano! Americano!"

Instantly, everyone sprang into action, and short but fierce fighting followed. American sailors, who had kept out of sight seemed to appear on deck out of nowhere. They boarded the *Philadelphia* and in a few minutes it was theirs. Some of the Moors escaped by jumping into the water and swimming ashore.

Decatur thought there was not time enough to put up the sails of the *Philadelphia* and try to escape with it, so he ordered his men to set it afire. This was done quickly.

As soon as the flames began to eat well into the frigate, the Americans returned to the little fifty-ton ketch on which they had entered the harbor. They had hardly set sail when the powder magazine of the *Philadelphia* blew up and flaming wreckage was scattered in all directions. Decatur and all his men escaped from the harbor, though they were under gunfire from

94

the forts on the shore, and one cannon ball actually went through the sails of their small craft.

Of this gallant performance at Tripoli, the British admiral, Lord Nelson, said, "It is the most bold and daring act of the age."

Six months later, Decatur was placed in command of a gunboat which took part in an attack on the Moorish fleet. He led a boarding party to the decks of an enemy vessel.

In the hand-to-hand fighting which followed, the young American officer found himself in savage combat with the Moorish captain. Decatur was wounded and his sword was broken, but after falling to the deck he grasped his pistol and shot the Moor.

At that very moment another Barbary pirate raised his long saber and was about to strike Decatur. Seeing the dangerous position of the fallen Decatur, a wounded seaman leapt in the path of the blow. The seaman was Reuben James. He suffered another serious wound but lived to enjoy the honor he deserved for bravely risking his own life in order to save his commander.

As a reward for his courage against the Barbary pirates, Decatur was made a captain in the Navy. He was given this commission when only twenty-five years of age, and was the youngest American ever to hold the rank.

The Barbary war was ended successfully in 1804, but eight years later a new and more serious war opened, this time with Great Britain. Commonly called the "War of 1812," the new conflict lasted two years and was fought largely at sea.

Captain Decatur took an active part in the fighting against the British. He was now in command of the *United States,* the vessel on which he first had sailed the Atlantic. On October 25, 1812, while cruising between the Canary Islands and the Azores, he came in sight of a British warship, the *Macedonian.*

With great speed the Americans unlashed and loaded their cannon. Cutlasses, pikes and other hand weapons were stacked near the masts, ready for use in case of boarding operations. Both vessels ran up their colors and, as soon as they came within range, they opened fire on each other. Close to

95

two hours of furious fighting followed, with broadsides being exchanged as fast as the guns could be loaded.

The British ship lost its mizzen topmast and its gaff halyards. Some of the wreckage fell on the mainsails and tangled with them. The *United States* lost its mizzen, the lowest square sail, but was not very badly damaged otherwise.

Finding that the guns of the *Macedonian* were outranged by those of the Americans, the British captain surrendered shortly before noon. He offered his sword to Decatur, but the American commander said: "Sir, I cannot receive the sword of a man who has so bravely defended his ship, but I will receive your hand."

Less than six weeks later Decatur reached New London, Connecticut, bringing with him the captive British warship. The victory caused great rejoicing among the American people, and Decatur was welcomed everywhere as a hero.

Toward the end of the war, Decatur himself was captured while boldly trying to run the blockade which had been set up by the enemy around New York Harbor. The British treated him with great courtesy and set him free a month later.

At the age of forty-one, Decatur fought a duel with another naval officer and fell mortally wounded by a pistol shot. His death was mourned throughout the nation.

MATTHEW CALBRAITH PERRY

MATTHEW CALBRAITH PERRY

Japan Opened Its Ports

BORN 1794—DIED 1858

Not often does the younger brother of a famous man also rise to fame, but that is what happened to Matthew Calbraith Perry. He was nine years younger than Oliver Hazard Perry, the American naval officer whose squadron won the Battle of Lake Erie in the War of 1812.

When that battle took place, Matthew was only nineteen years old. He was with his brother in the action, serving as a lieutenant on the *Lawrence* until the ship was sunk. Then, in company with other officers and men, he transferred to the *Niagara* during the very thick of the fighting. Thus began his long career in the American Navy which was to reach its high point when he sailed on a mission to Japan.

When war broke out between the United States and Mexico in 1846, Matthew Perry, after more than thirty years of duty on land and at sea, was put in command of several American warships during the siege and capture of the port of Vera Cruz.

Several years earlier, Matthew Perry had helped to design and to build steamships for the American Navy. Among them were the first frigates in the Navy, the *Missouri* and the *Mississippi*. Thus he earned for himself the title of "the Father of the Steam Navy."

The *Mississippi* was used by Perry in the most exciting and important adventure in his life, the so-called "opening of Japan." Up to that time the Japanese had tried to keep themselves apart from the western world. They had no desire to trade with white people, whether they came from North

99

America, Europe or anywhere else. They feared that, if they let foreigners come to their islands, there would be trouble in the end.

As a result of this course of action, the Japanese had learned little about new inventions which were starting to change the ways of life of people in other parts of the world. Indeed, they did not want to know about them.

From time to time, reports came to the western world about sailors who had been shipwrecked off the Japanese coasts and had been badly treated after reaching shore. Vessels which ran short of water in the Japanese area were not welcomed when they landed and asked for a fresh supply.

In 1846 two American ships under command of Commodore James Biddle had entered the Bay of Yedo, near Tokyo. No harm was done to the commodore or his men, but they were told firmly, "Go home and do not come back again!"

President Fillmore decided to make a strong effort to arrange some sort of treaty with Japan. He prepared a letter to the Emperor of Japan. This letter he gave to Commodore Perry and told him to take it to Japan. Late in the autumn of 1852, the commodore boarded the *Mississippi* at Annapolis, Maryland, and started on the long voyage.

In six months' time the vessel reached China where it was joined by another frigate and two sloops of war. In those days it was the custom for all steam-powered vessels to be fitted with sails as well as paddle-wheels. When Perry's little fleet traveled from China to Japan, the ships were propelled by wind as well as by steam power.

On July 8, 1853, the ships dropped anchor in the Bay of Yedo, twenty-seven miles from Tokyo. The Japanese who lived around the edge of the bay were astonished when they saw vessels with smokestacks. The sight was a strange one. Never before had they seen a steamship. The ships under Biddle, which had come seven years before, had been sailing vessels.

Small boats soon appeared alongside the American warships, but the men in them were not allowed to come on board. Perry wanted to make the natives feel the importance of this visit. Even when a "vice governor" appeared in a small boat, it was some time before the gangplank was lowered to permit him to step on the flagship. Even then he was not allowed to see the commodore. A lieutenant talked with him and told him why the Americans had come to Japan.

When the news of the arrival of the American fleet reached Tokyo, there was much excitement. A Japanese professor wrote about the event, saying, in part:

"No sooner had the black ships entered the bay than signal guns and rockets were discharged. Companies of soldiers moved along the shore from one guardhouse to another.

"The whole city of Yedo (or Tokyo) was in an uproar over the 'foreign invasion.' On every side women were to be seen running about with children in their arms. Some of the men carried their mothers on their backs. There was a great jumble of noise, with the clatter of armed warriors marching about, the jangle of carts, the tolling of bells, and the cries of women and children. A city of more than 1,000,000 people was in alarm."

On the next day the disturbed governor of the district came to the American ships, but the commodore would not talk with him, saying that the letter from President Fillmore to the Emperor would be given to no one lower in rank than a "Counselor of the Empire."

Finally, it was agreed that two Japanese princes would receive the President's letter. The notable event took place six days after the fleet had entered the bay.

One of the American warships fired a salute of thirteen guns as 300 naval officers, sailors and marines were lowered into launches and cutters to accompany Commodore Perry to the shore. After landing, the men drew up in parade formation. A seaman held a large American flag aloft as the men moved forward. Two boys carrying beautiful golden boxes wrapped in red cloth marched in front of the commodore. In each of the two boxes was a letter written on vellum. One letter introduced Perry and the other was the President's letter to the Emperor.

On either side of the commodore marched a Negro of huge size. The Japanese never before had seen anyone with black skin, and they looked upon these tall men with wonder.

A hall with hangings of violet silk and fine cotton had been prepared

101

for the meeting. When Perry and his men entered, the two princes rose, bowed and took their seats again. The commodore then gave a signal to the boys, and they stepped forward to deliver the golden boxes. At the close of the ceremony the American commander said that he would take his ships away from the harbor shortly, but would come back in the spring for the Emperor's answer.

Even before the spring season actually arrived, the Americans returned, this time with a fleet of six vessels. With three bands playing American music, Perry and 500 of his men marched to "Treaty House" in Yokohama. Three weeks were spent in meetings on shore while points in the treaty were being worked out and written down. During those weeks, the commodore gave to the Japanese officials a number of presents, which he had brought for them.

These gifts included clocks, two telegraph instruments, three lifeboats and, most important of all, a small railway train with tracks. The tracks were laid, and on them were placed the little locomotive with its tender and a single coach. Even a five-year-old boy would have had trouble squeezing inside the coach, but a full-grown Japanese was able to sit on the coach roof and take a ride. A fire was lighted to get up steam, and soon the locomotive was chugging around the track, which had been laid in a circle. The train made a speed as great as twenty miles an hour and supplied free rides to Japanese officials, one at a time.

The interest the Japanese took in the toy train may have played a part in bringing success to the American plans. In any case, a treaty was signed and sealed, and the American visitors were given presents such as dolls, baskets and umbrellas, along with 200 sacks of rice and 300 chickens. They were also invited to watch Japanese wrestling matches.

The treaty provided that Japan would allow trading at two of her seaports. The Japanese also promised good treatment to any Americans who might be shipwrecked in the area, and added that any American ship would be provided with water, wood and other supplies if it came to one of the two seaports.

Early in April, 1854, Perry sailed away from Japan. He had opened the door of trade with the people of the island empire. Later the Japanese also started to trade with other nations besides the United States.

The Japanese were to learn many things about the western world, and were to make their country up-to-date by using inventions from abroad. They were to learn about the machines of war which were used by white men, and were to imitate them. In less than a century they were to make war and to challenge the rule of the western nations over various parts of the Far East.

While on his way home, Commodore Perry had no idea of what the future held in store. To him, and to the world at large, the treaty he had made was simply a task well done.

Matthew Perry spent his last days in New York City. He died shortly before his sixty-fourth birthday, and holds an honored place in the history of the American Navy.

ROBERT E. LEE

ROBERT E. LEE

Soldier North and South

BORN 1807—DIED 1870

Where is the Mexican Army?

That question was asked time and again during the early months of the war between the United States and Mexico, which broke out in the spring of 1846. Before the end of the year, a few battles did take place, but there were more reports about Mexicans than there were actual Mexican soldiers.

A force of Americans, under General John E. Wool, was stationed at Encandata, near the borderline between Texas and Mexico, in December, 1846. Suddenly a report came to the general that a large Mexican Army was marching forward to attack the Americans.

There were no telephone lines in those days, so information could not be obtained in that way. The telegraph had been invented a few years before, but Wool and his men had no such help in their field headquarters. The only way to locate the Mexicans was through scouting.

The general asked for volunteers, and a thirty-nine-year-old captain from Virginia offered his services. His name was Robert E. Lee, and he was an army engineer. His skill had been of value in building bridges while Wool's army had advanced toward the Mexican border.

A cavalry escort was promised Lee, but it did not appear at the spot on the outer picket line where it was supposed to meet him. So Lee went forth with only a Mexican guide into the foothills of a mountain range.

After the two had ridden many miles, they caught sight of campfires on a

107

hill. Darkness had fallen, but the rays of the moon showed objects which looked like tents.

Many a scout would have hurried back to camp to announce that he had found the Mexican Army. But not Robert E. Lee! He wanted to make sure. His guide was very nervous, fearing that he might be captured and shot as a spy. So the captain told him to wait while he went on alone.

A closer view proved that the "tents" were small groups of sheep, and that the bonfires had been lighted by herdsmen. Lee talked with the herdsmen, and they told him that the Mexican Army was on the other side of the mountain range.

A full report was given to General Wool. Then Lee, after only three hours of rest, rode again to scout the enemy, this time with a cavalry escort. The Mexican Army was located more definitely, and the party returned safely to camp.

No battle followed immediately, but the incident showed something of the thorough method which Robert E. Lee would use on any mission. He was the son of General Henry Lee, the "Light-Horse Harry" who had won fame in the American Revolutionary War. As a young man he had gone to West Point, and had graduated with high honors. Now, for the first time, he was taking part in a war.

Within a few weeks of these scouting trips, transfer orders came to him. He was to join the forces of General Winfield Scott, and to take part in an expedition against a Mexican port. Mounting his faithful horse, a mare named Creole, he rode 250 miles to an assigned point, and there embarked on a ship which was to sail to the harbor of Vera Cruz.

The capture of the harbor of Vera Cruz proved a simple matter, since there were several American warships with the transport vessels. After the landing, however, there remained a walled city with a fortified castle to capture.

Lee was one of the officers whom Scott consulted to learn the best method of attack. He was given the special task of preparing a battery with cannon borrowed from the American warships.

The cannon were brought ashore and, under the captain's directions, the battery was made ready with great care so that it should not be seen by the Mexicans before it was finished. Trenches were cut near the cannon. Some of the sailors who were to man the battery grumbled about digging ditches instead of fighting, but later they were glad to be able to escape Mexican rifle bullets and cannon balls by crouching in these very ditches.

When Lee at length ordered the battery to open fire, it did more damage than any other American battery, in fact more than all others combined. The walls of Vera Cruz gave way, and sections of the city were blasted. After three days of fighting the Mexicans surrendered.

Before the Mexican war was over, Robert E. Lee had advanced beyond the rank of captain. While the American troops were proceeding from Vera Cruz to Mexico City, he was made major, then lieutenant-colonel. He finished the war as a colonel.

The march to Mexico's capital was made in part through mountain passes. Lee's engineering skill was brought into play time and again. General Scott praised his work highly in his reports to the War Department in Washington.

A few years after the end of the war, Colonel Lee was placed in charge of West Point, acting as its superintendent for three years from 1852 to 1855. The students liked and respected him. There was careful discipline, but the superintendent showed himself to be not only fair but also kindly.

After leaving West Point, Lee had charge of American cavalrymen in lands between the Arkansas and Rio Grande rivers. His task was to guard the settlers against attacks by Apache and Comanche Indians.

Returning to Virginia in 1859, Colonel Lee was called upon to capture a party of white men led by John Brown. These men had come into the state to excite the Negroes to rebel. They had broken into a government arsenal at Harper's Ferry, and had seized weapons which they planned to use in arming the slaves. With a company of Marines, the colonel surrounded Brown and his men in the armory's engine-house, and ordered them to surrender. When they refused, the Marines battered down a door. Brown surrendered after several of his party had been killed or wounded. All the white hostages, whom Brown had held and threatened to kill, were set free.

Lee has left us no information as to how he felt about this performance of a duty. We do know, however, what he thought about negro slavery. He had freed the slaves who had been left to him by his father and mother, and he had said that he believed slavery to be wrong. Yet he was against the idea of taking slaves away from their masters by force. He believed that peaceful means would, at length, end slavery.

During his young manhood, Lee had been impressed by a slave uprising led by a Negro named Nat Turner. This man had been joined by sixty other slaves and had armed them with stolen weapons. Moving from plantation to plantation, they had killed thirteen men, eighteen women and twenty-four children. At length Turner had been captured and hanged along with nineteen of his men. The little rebellion had been stamped out, but many persons saw in it a proof of danger if Negroes in general should rise in rebellion.

As it turned out, the Negro slaves did very little fighting even after the outbreak of the Civil War. Most of them seemed to be content to stay at home and work on their old plantations.

While the American Civil War was brewing, Robert E. Lee had a hard time deciding what to do. It appears that he was offered the post of commander of the Union forces. Had he accepted, the war probably would have been a short one. His great skill both in strategy and tactics no doubt would have won battles which the Union generals were not able to win.

"I believe in union of the states," said Lee, "but union is not worthwhile if force must be used to maintain it."

Instead of accepting promotion, Lee resigned his place in the American army. He said he would not again raise his sword unless directed to do so by the State of Virginia. Thus he made the hard, sad choice of standing by his state instead of the nation.

The story of the Civil War is in part a record of the work of Robert E. Lee. Becoming Commander in Chief of the Confederate forces, he proved himself one of the great generals of history. His armies did not equal those of the North in size, but time and again they were victorious in battle. They were handled in a masterful way, not only by Lee but also by some of the generals under him, such as Beauregard and Stonewall Jackson.

Lee at all times did his best to keep the Southern soldiers provided with

110

enough food and clothing, as well as arms and ammunition. In spite of the shortage of factories in the South, the great task of supplying the army was carried out very well within the limits of what could be obtained.

The soldiers of the South came to love and trust their commander. They fought and died with the feeling that he was doing his best. His keen mind saw problems, and solved them. His knowledge of engineering was of special importance in fitting him to meet and overcome certain obstacles.

Yet, with all his brilliance as a general, Lee found that his armies were being worn down. Supplies were failing to come, and large Union armies under Grant, Sherman and Sheridan were driving into the South. When he saw that defeat was ahead, Lee decided to surrender. He felt that there no longer was good reason to sacrifice the lives of more soldiers by dragging out the conflict.

So it came about that General Lee signed terms of surrender at Appomattox Courthouse, Virginia, on April 9, 1865. A legend grew up that he offered his sword to General Grant but that Grant refused to accept it. That legend has been disputed with good reason. The terms of surrender provided that Southern officers need not give up their sidearms. Lee kept his sword, and it may well be that in later years it reminded him of a painful duty which he had performed as well as he could.

After the war, Lee was made President of Washington College at Lexington, Virginia. He held this position until his death at the age of sixty-three. The name of the college later was changed in his honor, and it became Washington and Lee University.

Even in the North, people came to admire General Lee. As the anger aroused by warfare died down, it grew plain to many of his former enemies that he had acted simply as he believed to be right when he stood by his state in the conflict.

ULYSSES S. GRANT

ULYSSES S. GRANT

Commander of the Union Army

BORN 1822—DIED 1885

A N ERROR MADE BY a congressman helped to change the name of a general! The congressman was asked to suggest the name of a young man for the United States Military Academy at West Point. He was filling out the necessary papers when he paused over the lad's middle name. He knew the parents of young Grant fairly well. He had always heard the boy called Ulysses, but he was not certain about his middle name.

"It must be Simpson," he decided, "since his mother's maiden name was Simpson." So he wrote "Ulysses Simpson Grant" on the West Point papers.

Meanwhile the boy himself, Hiram Ulysses Grant, was helping his father on the family farm near Georgetown, Ohio. He had been born at Point Pleasant in a nearby county of Ohio in 1822. During his boyhood his family had called him Ulysses instead of Hiram, but others had given him the nickname of "Useless," because, they said, he did not like to work.

Despite that nickname, Ulysses had done a great deal of work on the farm. He had plowed the ground, sown the seed, and reaped the grain. Indeed he had become rather stoop-shouldered, and this seems to have been due to the hard toil.

Few persons thought of the youth as being likely to succeed in life, but he had one talent which stood out. He could handle horses well, no matter how balky they might be. He proved this time and again.

One day a small circus came to Georgetown, and the owner of the circus offered a prize of five dollars to any boy who could stay on the back of a trick pony for five minutes. Many of the local farm boys tried to win the prize, but each was thrown in a hurry. The pony had no saddle or bridle, and even its mane had been cut off. The pony had been taught to rear on its hind legs, and to do other things to shake off any would-be rider. At length Ulysses tried his fortune. Wrapping his arms around the animal's neck, he held on tightly, and won the five dollars.

When young Grant learned that he was to go to West Point, he was seventeen years old. He packed his belongings, and, before he left the initials "H.U.G." were printed on his trunk. On his way to the academy, he began to think about those initials, worrying lest his classmates might give him the nickname of "Hug." On his arrival, therefore, he reversed his names and signed himself Ulysses Hiram Grant. An official of the school, upon looking at the papers, said that a Ulysses Simpson Grant had been expected, and that the records could not be changed unless the papers were sent to the army offices in Washington for correction.

"Very well," said Grant, "I will adopt Simpson as my middle name!"

Thus it came about that the future general and future American president changed his name at the age of seventeen. His classmates were quick to notice the initials "U.S." and decided that they ought to stand for Uncle Sam. So Sam he was called during his years at West Point.

Grant passed his courses at West Point, but did not stand very high in his class at graduation. Only in the study of mathematics had he shown any special ability.

Shortly after leaving the academy, Grant fought in the Mexican War. He saw action in several battles, and was promoted to the rank of captain.

A few years after the close of the war, Grant dropped out of the Army. He had formed the habit of drinking liquor. Complaints had been made that this habit was so strong that he should not be an officer in the American Army.

While still in the army, Grant had been married, and now he made his home with his wife in a rather large log-cabin near St. Louis, Missouri. There he stayed for six years, earning his living by farming and selling houses and land. In 1860 he moved to Galena, Illinois, and became a clerk in a leather goods store which his father had started.

Anyone who had followed Grant's career up to that point might have said that he "never would amount to much." Indeed some persons in Galena called him "a has-been army officer."

Soon his whole life was to change with the outbreak of the American Civil War in 1861. His feelings were stirred, and he felt that he must do something to help save the Union. Quickly he offered his services in drilling a company of volunteer soldiers at Galena.

The war was less than two months old when Grant was made a colonel in command of a regiment of volunteers. He led his men into Missouri, where fighting was going on between men of the North and the South.

As a colonel of the volunteer regiment, Grant soon showed signs of the military skill which was to make his name so well known later. After a few battles in Missouri, he made a quick march to Paducah, Kentucky, and occupied that town a few hours before it would have been reached by a Confederate Army. The importance of Paducah was due to its being at the junction point of the Tennessee and Ohio rivers. All through the war, Grant made a special point of getting control of waterways which could be used for sending supplies.

Early in 1862 Grant, who had been made a brigadier general, advanced with the Union armies up the valleys of the Cumberland and Tennessee rivers. In this campaign he captured Fort Donelson, with the 15,000 Confederate soldiers stationed there.

In the following year, Grant was in command when one of the great victories of the Civil War, the capture of Vicksburg, was won. The city of Vicksburg is in Mississippi, and it was a stronghold of the Confederate states. Located on a sharp bend of the Mississippi River, it could stop the passage of Union ships up and down that great waterway. Vicksburg was captured on the Fourth of July, 1863, and 29,491 men surrendered.

By this time Grant seemed to be on the high road to success, but his old enemy, an appetite for strong drink, was with him still. He fought against this foe, and in large measure was able to defeat it. A letter on the subject

117

was sent to him by a member of his staff, John A. Rawlins. In the letter Rawlins pleaded with the brigadier general to think of the lives of the soldiers under his command. Instead of growing angry toward Rawlins, Grant took the letter in good part, and tried harder to follow sober habits.

Four months after the capture of Vicksburg, Grant and his men were in the eastern part of the state of Tennessee where they won a new victory. As a result of the Battle of Chattanooga, a Confederate Army was put to flight.

News of Grant's victories did not escape President Lincoln in Washington. Most other Union generals had failed to win important battles, but here was a man from the West who could hew a path to his goal. On February 26, 1864, Lincoln named him to command all Union forces and gave him the advanced rank of lieutenant general.

General Grant now planned a strong drive to split the forces of the South. William T. Sherman, a brigadier general, was given orders to capture Atlanta and march through Georgia to the Atlantic coast. These plans were crowned with final success when Savannah surrendered to Sherman on December 21, 1864.

Meanwhile Grant had been driving against General Robert E. Lee, who was in personal command of the main Confederate Army. This army was in Virginia, and was encamped in and around Richmond, the capital.

Advancing into Virginia, General Grant met the Confederate Army in battle after battle. The Union forces more than once met defeat, but Grant drove on with his campaign. He gained control of points along the James and Shenandoah rivers, and was slowly but surely hemming Lee in and wearing down his army.

The supplies of the Confederates were running low. Tired and hungry, Lee's soldiers waited for orders. At last, on April 7, 1865, Grant sent a letter to Lee, saying that he thought it was useless for the Southern Army to resist further. Lee replied by asking what terms would be offered in case of surrender.

Other letters were exchanged, and on April 9 the two generals met at Appomattox Courthouse, about eighty miles west of Richmond. One general went there as the victor, and the other as the leader of a lost cause.

118

If Ulysses Simpson Grant had been a man of small mind, he could have used that meeting to speak cutting words to his fallen foe. As it was, he treated Lee with respect and kindliness. The two men talked over the terms of surrender, and at length signed the papers which put those terms into writing.

On his part, Lee gave no clear sign of how he felt. He spoke no words to show that he was glad that the bitter struggle was over, nor did he display any outward sign of sadness. By the terms of surrender, all Confederate officers and soldiers were free to go back to their homes, under promise that they would not again take up arms.

Before the meeting was over, General Grant spoke about the horses of the many Confederate cavalrymen who were not officers. He said that these men, too, could take their horses home for use in the spring plowing.

The surrender of Lee, with his army of about 25,000 men, marked the real end of the American Civil War. There were, indeed, other Confederate soldiers still in the field, but their surrender soon followed. No more were Americans to face each other on blood-stained battlefields of their own country.

Three years after the close of the war, Grant's friends chose him as a candidate for President of the United States. He had taken little interest in politics up to that time, but he was elected President in 1868, and again in 1872.

After giving up the office of President, Grant made a trip around the world, visiting Great Britain, India, China, Japan and other countries. Shortly before his death on July 23, 1885, he finished writing an interesting book, "Personal Memoirs," which told the story of his life. He was buried in New York City, his body being placed in a tomb near the Hudson River.

ADMIRAL DEWEY

ADMIRAL DEWEY

Hero of Manila Bay

BORN 1837—DIED 1917

WHEN ABRAHAM LINCOLN was elected President of the United States in 1860, a young American named George Dewey was starting a career in the Navy.

Dewey had been a student at the Naval Academy in Annapolis. His work there had been so poor at first that he ranked third from last in the class. Such low marks were far from pleasing to him, so he set his mind to his studies from that time onward. By the time he was graduated, he was fifth from the top!

The start of the Civil War found Dewey aboard a side-wheel frigate called the *Mississippi*. He was at first an officer of low rank but as the war went on, he rose to one higher grade after another, partly because of the transfer of his senior officers to other ships. When only twenty-three years old, he was made executive officer of the *Mississippi*, and the captain spoke of him as one of the best assistants who had ever served under his command.

Shortly afterward Dewey took part in one of the important naval actions of the Civil War. This was the passage of a Union fleet into the Mississippi River, right past the powerful forts which guarded New Orleans near the mouth of the river. Admiral Farragut was in command of the fleet, and Dewey was aboard the side-wheeler on which he was executive officer. During that night of danger, he had charge of the piloting, and gave orders as to how the ship should be steered. His captain had turned this task over to him, saying that Dewey's eyes were sharper than his own.

As the *Mississippi* steamed upstream, Dewey suddenly spotted an approaching low-lying boat which had much the outline of a turtle's back. It was the Confederate ram, *Manasses*. Dewey headed his ship straight at the ram, but the Confederate vessel dodged aside and struck the *Mississippi* a glancing blow near the paddle-wheel. Little damage was done, but if it had not been for the quick turn made by Dewey, his ship probably would have been destroyed.

Toward dawn, Dewey sighted the *Manasses* coming back for another attack. This time the ram was damaged by heavy broadsides from the Union vessel and was driven aground. Those of the crew who were able to do so scrambled ashore shortly before their ship was set ablaze and destroyed.

After the close of the Civil War, Dewey stayed in the service of the Navy, and rose to the rank of captain. During the following years of peace, he studied the art of naval warfare, giving special attention to the geography of the Far East. Later he was to put the knowledge he had gained to good use.

In 1897 the post of commander of the American fleet in the Pacific Ocean fell vacant, and Dewey was named commodore of that section of the Navy. He sailed to Hongkong, China, where the fleet was stationed at the time.

On April 24 in the following year, a state of war was declared between Spain and the United States. The news was telegraphed to Dewey, and on the very next day he received an official order to attack the Philippine Islands, which then made up the larger part of Spain's colonial empire.

The outbreak of war was no surprise to Dewey. The American battleship *Maine* had blown up in the harbor of Havana, Cuba, two months before, and bitter feeling existed between Spaniards and Americans. When he received the order to attack, Dewey already had left Hongkong, and had set up a base at Mirs Bay, a nearby harbor on the Chinese coast. The sailors in his fleet had been put through the most careful drilling, and he felt that they were ready for action.

The fleet was headed toward Manila Bay, chief stronghold of the Spaniards in the Philippines. This harbor was guarded by a Spanish fleet and

124

also by strong land batteries. One important battery base was on the small island of Corregidor. It seemed almost impossible for any force to break through such strong defenses.

In five days, Dewey came within sight of the harbor, but he ordered his fleet to wait for darkness. When night fell, the signal was given to steam ahead. Mines had been laid at the harbor entrance by the Spaniards, but fortunately the warships did not strike any of them as the entry was made.

While the American fleet was sailing toward the entrance to the harbor, the Spanish admiral and his wife were giving a ball in the city. Many officers in his fleet were guests at the ball, and were dancing while the Americans were coming to the attack!

The officers in command of the Spanish forts were on the alert, however, and the forts at the entrance to the bay fired at Dewey's fleet shortly after midnight. The American ships replied to the fire, but the main object was to reach the enemy fleet, some miles distant in the big harbor. The battle started in earnest at daybreak on May 1. The Spanish admiral, Montojo, and most of his officers had returned to the fleet soon after the first cannon in the forts were fired.

The guns of Corregidor and other batteries blazed away at the Americans, but Dewey headed for the fleet. At a range of two and a half miles, he gave the first order to fire at a Spanish ship. Broadsides were exchanged by the fleets, but the American gunners proved to be far better marksmen.

A Spanish torpedo boat was sunk, and Montojo's flagship was struck and set afire. The admiral and his crew quickly took to small boats, and rowed to another warship.

Suddenly the American fire ceased, and Dewey's fleet turned and steamed to the other side of the bay. The Spaniards supposed that the Americans were going away to make repairs, but that was not the case. Dewey had received a report that his ammunition was running low, and he wanted to check the supply while out of range of the enemy. Besides, it was time for the American sailors to have breakfast. The report later was spread that the Americans had taken time out just for breakfast, but the meal was not nearly so important as the check on ammunition.

125

Within a few hours the American warships returned to finish the battle. More enemy ships were sunk, and the Spanish admiral sent up the white flag of surrender shortly after noon.

On the American side not a single ship had been lost, and not a single sailor was killed in action. Eight Americans were listed as wounded.

The Battle of Manila Bay helped to decide the Spanish-American War, and it also gave Dewey widespread fame. Shortly afterward he was made a rear admiral, then was honored with the title of Admiral of the Navy.

Dewey was in his eightieth year at the time of his death in 1917. He ranks as one of the great admirals in American naval history.

FERDINAND FOCH

FERDINAND FOCH

He Commanded the Allied Armies

BORN 1851—DIED 1929

DURING THE FIRST World War from 1914 to 1918, no general won higher honor for his skill than Ferdinand Foch. Yet in the midst of that war there was a time when his command was taken from him, and he had to serve merely as an inspector. He was, indeed, in a state of disgrace!

Foch was born in the small city of Tarbes in southern France. This city is on the northern side of the Pyrenees, the great mountain range which divides France from Spain.

There were three sons in the Foch family. One son became a lawyer, like his father, another became a Jesuit priest, and the third went into the army.

During his boyhood, Ferdinand showed a deep interest in stories about the life of Napoleon. In his mind this conquering general was a great hero, and the lad read all the books about him that he could find. For a long time Napoleon's life was a pattern for his own. We are told that one day he said to his father: "I have been trying to find out what Napoleon did in his school holidays! But I cannot learn whether or not he went fishing. I would be glad if I found out that he liked to fish."

Ferdinand was nineteen years of age and was at college when he heard about the outbreak of the Franco-Prussian War in 1870. Quickly he offered his services and was accepted in the French Army. He was anxious to do his part in helping his country to make a stand against the invasion of the Prussians. He went into training as an infantry soldier but, before he could join the army in actual fighting, the war was over. France suffered a severe defeat.

The rout of the armies of France led to the loss of the territory of Alsace-Lorraine. This blow stirred the youth, and he began to feel that France must later get back what had been taken away. Speaking to a friend, he said, "I must become one of the liberators of France."

Shortly after his twentieth birthday Foch went to Paris to continue his studies at a school of science and engineering. He became especially interested in science, and when he finished his courses in Paris he was well prepared for work in the Army. Later he studied in a school for officers, and was made a second lieutenant of artillery.

Rising to the rank of captain in 1878, he continued to serve in the Army. At the age of forty-three he became a professor at the War College of France, and for years afterward taught young army officers how to plan campaigns and fight battles. His lectures were published in two books, "The Conduct of War" and "Principles of War."

In 1907, at the age of fifty-six, Foch was made head of the War College of France. Then, in 1911, he was placed in command of a division in the French Army, and soon afterward he was put in charge of an entire army corps, with headquarters at Nancy, in northern France.

In the years which followed, Foch rose swiftly in army rank, becoming colonel, brigadier general and then full general. His ideas and his methods began to attract attention of army men in other countries.

In October, 1910, an aged British army officer, Lord Roberts, gave a speech in Quebec, Canada, and made this remarkable statement:

"I do not hesitate to affirm that we shall have a frightful war in Europe, and that England and France will have the hardest experience of their existence. They will, in fact, see defeat very near, but the war will finally be won by the genius of a French general named Ferdinand Foch."

Lord Roberts died two months after the outbreak of the first World War, so he could not watch the course of the war to see how truly his words would be borne out by events.

Foch was not quite sixty-three years of age when he first led his troops into battle against the Germans in 1914. Although he had command of the Twentieth Army Corps, other Frenchmen had higher rank during the early period of the war. General Joffre watched his work during a retreat and counter-attack in the fall of 1914, and promoted him to the command of one of the French armies. Soon afterward Foch helped to stem the tide of the German onrush and to bring victory to the Allies in the first Battle of the Marne.

The next order given to Foch was to head off a German drive toward the English Channel, with the help of the British and Belgian armies. The task was carried out well. The Germans were checked, and the French general showed clearly how much help the Allied armies could be to one another.

The war, however, dragged on and on. German generals also were skillful, and were in command of well-trained, hard-fighting troops. By the summer of 1916, when the Battle of the Somme was raging, the Allies had met with more setbacks than victories. There was a feeling in France that a change in the high command was needed. General Joffre was removed from his post at the head of the French forces. At the same time General Foch, replaced by a new officer, was sent to Senlis, a town northeast of Paris, "on a mission of inspection." It was reported that he needed a rest, but it was well known that he was being given less important work to do.

In the spring of the next year, Foch was called back into active service as chief of staff under General Pétain. In this position he came into close contact with British and Italian generals, and was admired for his firm will and quick grasp of military plans and methods. In the dark days suffered by the Allies early in 1918, the feeling grew strong that all the Allied armies in France should be under the command of a single general. For that task General Foch was chosen. The honor was great, indeed.

With a sure hand, Foch met the new German offensive, and proved to the British and Americans that he could rush troops to their aid in moments of stress. From the British and Americans he obtained equal co-operation. At last, the Germans were checked in the Battle of the Aisne and the Second Battle of the Marne.

Foch was not content merely with checking the foe. His object was to end the war by a powerful drive of all forces under his command. On August 8, 1918, he ordered the start of this great drive against the enemy. It was successful. The Germans were hurled back to the Hindenburg Line, which ran through northern France.

In less than a month the Hindenburg Line was cracked in one section, and Allied soldiers were pushing forward at many points. Foch decided to draw a circle around the main German forces on the Western Front, and this plan was working well early in November. Before the circle could be completed, however, the German generals asked for an Armistice. A meeting was arranged, and, on November 8, a group of Germans came to see Foch to talk about the terms of surrender. Three days later—at the eleventh hour of the eleventh day of the eleventh month of 1918—the Armistice became a fact. The most bloody war the white race had ever suffered was declared at an end, so far as fighting was concerned.

Three months before the Armistice, Foch had been given the title of Marshal of France. With the victorious ending of the war, he was hailed in all Allied countries. Great Britain gave him the honorary title of British Field Marshal, and he also became Marshal of Poland. He was made a member of the French Academy, and in 1919 he marched at the head of thousands of Allied soldiers through the Arch of Triumph in Paris. Later he made a tour of the United States, and gave talks in several cities. His death occurred on March 20, 1929, and his body was laid to rest in Paris, near the tomb of Napoleon, the hero of his boyhood.

GENERAL PERSHING

GENERAL PERSHING

Commander of the A.E.F.

BORN 1860—

One year before the outbreak of the American Civil War an infant was born near the little frontier town of Laclede, Missouri. The father was John F. Pershing, and the child was given the name of John Joseph.

While John was growing up, his father earned a living in several ways. For some years he worked for a railway company, helping to lay tracks and to manage a number of laborers. He also spent some time farming a strip of land, and, when he was able to do so, he bought a store in Laclede and went into business.

John was one of nine children. Like the other boys in his family, he did a great deal of work on the farm when he was free from his studies at school. Although he was not a brilliant pupil, he liked the idea of becoming educated, and in the later years of his youth he made special efforts toward that goal.

When only seventeen years of age, John became a school teacher. His pupils were Negro children. Soon he was given a new nickname. He had been called "Jack" by many of his friends, but now some of them started calling him "Black Jack" because of his colored pupils.

To teach school at that time was, for him, just a means to an end. Young Pershing wanted to save money so that he could attend a training school for teachers, for further education. In a short time he became a student at the Kirksville Normal School in Missouri.

135

In the village store kept by his father there was a post office as well. One day the post office was robbed, with the result that John's father was called upon to make good the loss of government money. We are told that the son came to the rescue and gave his father money which he had earned and saved for his further schooling.

John Pershing's education was by no means at an end, however. Learning that an examination for West Point was to be held, he made a trip to Trenton, Missouri, and was among the eighteen young men who competed. His score was highest of all.

Pershing was delighted to be sent to West Point. He joined in all the activities and became a part of the life at the Academy. Although his class work was not excellent, it was satisfactory. Among his classmates he was very popular and soon became a leader. He was chosen president of his class before he was graduated in 1886.

As a young cavalry officer in the United States Army, Pershing saw service against a tribe of Apache Indians who were making trouble in the southwestern part of the United States. Soon afterward he was sent to South Dakota to command the soldiers who were helping to put down an uprising of the Sioux Indians.

Pershing was twenty-nine years of age when he showed that bullets were not always the best answer to angry Indians. Receiving word that Zuni warriors were about to attack a band of trouble-making white men, he hurried to the rescue. Instead of opening fire on the Indians, he talked with their leaders and asked them what was wrong. When complaints about the white men were made, he promised that if the Indians would settle the matter peacefully he would see that justice was done. An agreement was reached, and the trouble was ended without the firing of a single shot. The second lieutenant had taken the trouble to learn the facts and had acted on them with good results.

In 1891 Pershing became an instructor of military science at the University of Nebraska. At the same time, during the next two years, he spent his free hours in the study of law, and was graduated as a lawyer. Again he proved how strong was his desire to become educated.

War with Spain broke out in 1898, and Pershing went to Cuba and served through the Santiago campaign. His commander in Cuba later said that he was "the coolest man under fire" he had ever seen.

By the time he was sent to serve in Cuba, Pershing had risen to the rank of captain. Then, after further important service in the Philippine Islands, he was promoted to the rank of major. Three years later, in 1906, he became a brigadier general.

During the Russo-Japanese War, Pershing acted as a military observer of battles between the Russians and Japanese, and his report on the fighting was called "clear-cut and valuable." Following the war, he was made military governor of the Moro tribesmen in the Philippines.

After returning to the United States, General Pershing was sent to the Mexican border in 1915. Following the death of General Frederick Funston two years later, he was promoted to full command of American troops in that area.

Few generals in history have seen action in such widely separated parts of the world as John J. Pershing did. He had served on the western plains of the United States, in Cuba and in the Philippines. His greatest fame was to come to him after the United States entered the first World War in 1917.

In June, 1917, two months after the United States declared war on Germany, Pershing was sent to France in full command of the American Expeditionary Force, or "A.E.F.," as it was commonly called. As soon as he reached France, he began to study the needs of American soldiers and used his driving force to get them ready for battle. He was in active command of American troops in their victory at St. Mihiel. Later he directed what came to be known as the Meuse-Argonne operation. This was not a single battle but a series of attacks and counter-attacks stretching over a period of six weeks.

The Meuse-Argonne fighting was opened on September 26, 1918, and was centered in the area between the Meuse River and the Argonne Forest, northeast of Paris. At the outset the Americans had 180 tanks, 800 airplanes and 1,800 cannon. With reinforcements arriving in October, Pershing was able to send more than 1,000,000 soldiers into the conflict.

Day by day the struggle went on, both sides losing heavily. The Americans lost many thousands in killed and wounded, but they drove the German Army back and captured great numbers of prisoners. The Meuse-Argonne operation struck Germany such fierce blows that it could not recover in that area, and the Armistice soon followed on November 11.

Ten months after the Armistice, Pershing was confirmed in the rank of full general in the United States Army. Only four men in American history had held this rank before him—Washington, Grant, Sherman and Sheridan.

In 1921 Pershing was named chief-of-staff of the United States Army, and, while he held this office, he made every effort to build up a new and better framework for its forces. Following the Japanese attack on Pearl Harbor on December 7, 1941, and the entrance of the United States into the second World War, Pershing's advice was asked on many questions important to the carrying out of military operations.

LEADERS IN THE
SECOND WORLD WAR

LEADERS IN THE SECOND WORLD WAR

THE STORY OF General George C. Marshall, the Army Chief of Staff in Washington, might be started when he found himself in "the awkward squad." In the year 1897, the sixteen-year-old youth from Uniontown, Pennsylvania, entered the Virginia Military Institute. He was "lean, shy and gawky," and, because he was among the cadets who did not get along well at drilling, he was put in the so-called awkward squad.

That was just at the start. Four years later this youth graduated at the head of his class! When a man or boy shows skill in turning defeat into victory, he has a real quality of greatness. Marshall showed that quality in his personal life at the Virginia Military Institute, and in later years as a military leader.

Good-natured, but quick to set things right, he became a great leader not through daring deeds on the battlefield but because he could plan so skillfully and could see his plans carried out.

Even during the first World War, when he went to France as an army captain, Marshall was, for the most part, far from the smoke of battle. His superior officers had found in him a man who could take charge of important operations for them at headquarters. He was only thirty-six years old when that war broke out, but he had already been spoken of as "the greatest military genius of America since Stonewall Jackson." The comment was made after Marshall, as a young lieutenant, had taken charge of Army maneuvers in the Philippines, and had issued a series of brilliant orders.

Marshall's major exploit in the first World War was to move more than 500,000 American troops from one French battlefield to another without letting the Germans learn what had happened until they were suffering defeat.

Marshall became a colonel before the Armistice of 1918. Other promotions came to him after the return of peace. He rose in the Army until at length he was made Chief of Staff at Washington. Since 1939 he has held the rank of general. The Chief of Staff must make decisions which bring success or failure to American forces all over the world.

Carrying out the plans made by General Marshall were Eisenhower, fighting in Europe, and MacArthur, in the Pacific.

Dwight Eisenhower, while he was a young man in Kansas, wanted to go to the Naval Academy at Annapolis, where a friend of his was a teacher. However, by the time he had made up his mind to do so, he learned that he was a few months too old to enter.

If Eisenhower had gone to the Naval Academy, he very likely would have risen to be captain of a warship, or possibly an admiral. Yet, whatever honor he might have won on the sea, he would not have been in line to lead the land invasion of the Allies in North Africa, Sicily and Italy. Neither would he have been likely to command the Allied forces gathered in Great Britain to storm western Europe in 1944.

Dwight David Eisenhower was born in Denison, a small city in northern Texas, on October 14, 1890. Although he was a Texan by birth, his family returned to Kansas while he was still a tiny tot, and settled at Abilene. The family lived in an old house in the city's outskirts. The grounds around the house were large enough for the Eisenhowers to plant a large garden, and to stable a horse and a cow. As soon as he was old enough to do so, Dwight helped his older brothers milk the cow, weed the garden, and "hitch up" the horse. Dwight was the third son, but three more children, all boys, were born in later years.

Dwight Eisenhower had just passed his twenty-first birthday when he found that he was too old to become a student at Annapolis. So he changed his plans and took examinations for the West Point Military Academy instead. He passed with a high grade and before long became a cadet.

Graduating from West Point in 1915, young Eisenhower was in army service a year after the first World War broke out. Less than two years after his graduation, the United States entered the conflict. He was not sent abroad, but served as a captain, helping to train soldiers for foreign service. In 1918 he was placed in command of a tank camp in Pennsylvania. He became keenly interested in tanks, an invention of the first World War which was to be most important in the second World War.

Not content with what he had learned about tanks in the field, Eisenhower became a student at the Army Tank School after the war was over. He graduated from that school, and later attended the Army War College. He was thirty-nine years old when he finished the War College courses.

Known by the nickname of "Ike," Eisenhower proved time and again his belief that a man should never feel himself "too old to learn." During service in the Philippine Islands under General Douglas MacArthur, he studied flying, and at the age of forty-seven was granted a pilot's license.

Eisenhower returned from the Philippines in 1940 and, in the following year, he became a brigadier-general. Then, in 1942, he was made head of the War Plans Division of the Army General Staff at Washington.

This high office was of special importance because the United States had entered the second World War. Great confidence in Eisenhower was shown by President Franklin D. Roosevelt, and during the course of 1942 he was named by President Roosevelt and Prime Minister Winston Churchill of Great Britain to command the Allied forces. Under his leadership the Allies captured Tunisia, Sicily, Sardinia and Corsica, and the southern third of Italy.

Partly because of his victories in the Mediterranean area, General Eisenhower was chosen late in 1943 to command all Allied land, sea and air forces in the liberation of western Europe. In bidding farewell to his troops on the Southern Front, he promised to meet them in the heart of Europe after the opening of the Western Front. In February, 1944, he was made a full general. He was in supreme command of the Allied forces which landed on the coast of Normandy in France on June 6, 1944. He told his men: "We will accept nothing less than full victory."

143

Meanwhile other generals were giving their best to the cause of the United Nations. Among the British leaders who won important victories are General Sir Harold Alexander and General Sir Bernard Montgomery. Together they planned and carried out a successful drive against German and Italian forces. pushing them from the Egyptian border into Tunisia in 1942 and 1943. When the Allied assault began in France, General Montgomery was in charge of the land forces which pushed inland from the coast of Normandy.

In Russia skillful generals directed the fighting of great armies which stood in the path of Hitler's furious efforts to spread German power eastward. In 1943 these armies began to strike with mighty power against the Germans, making them retreat toward their own borders. By the summer of 1944 the Russian armies had driven inside East Prussia, Poland, Latvia and Lithuania. Semyon Timoshenko, Nikolai Vatutin, Ivan S. Konev, and Gregory K. Zhukov are among the Russian generals who at one time or another have won praise as outstanding leaders, but history may reveal Josef Stalin as the guiding military genius who first halted and then reversed Hitler's sweep through Europe.

In the year which followed the Japanese attack on Pearl Harbor, on December 7, 1941, the foremost general in the minds of Americans was Douglas MacArthur. Stationed in the Philippines at the head of an army of moderate size, he met the invasion of the Japanese with coolness and courage. After his small air fleet had been whittled down and broken, he gave up the city of Manila, but kept his army together during a retreat into the Bataan Peninsula. The Americans fought heroically and stubbornly each step of the way, but Japanese soldiers came pouring into the battle area, and finally forced the Americans to make their last stand on the fortified, but small, island of Corregidor.

Finding that the defense of the Philippines was hopeless, the men at Washington in charge of American war plans ordered MacArthur to leave the scene of battle and go to Australia. As he left his cornered troops, he made a promise that he would return later to free the Filipinos from Japanese rule.

As commander of Allied forces in a large section of the Pacific, MacArthur in 1943 and 1944 directed the campaign against the Japanese. American,

British and Australian soldiers, sailors and marines under his command freed New Guinea from Japanese troops, and also drove them from most of the smaller islands north and east of New Guinea.

In December, 1941, Admiral Ernest Joseph King was made Commander in Chief of the entire American fleet, almost the same place as Marshall's in the army command. Two years older than Marshall, King graduated from the Naval Academy at Annapolis in 1901, the same year Marshall finished his studies at Virginia Military Institute. King, however, had seen service as a midshipman in the Spanish-American War before starting at Annapolis.

Born at Lorain, Ohio, in 1878, King rose step by step to the highest command of the American fleet. He became rear admiral in 1933, and vice admiral in 1938. In 1940 he was Commander in Chief of the Atlantic fleet, and next year was given the rank of full admiral. Largely because of his skill, the American Navy made an excellent record after the Japanese attack on Pearl Harbor.

On the land and on the sea, men with brilliant minds were given the task of directing the hard fighting of the second World War. Although military men give their thoughts to ways of winning victories, it would be a mistake to suppose that all of them, or even the majority, approve of the idea of trying to settle quarrels by warfare. In modern days, at least, the common opinion among them has been in agreement with such generals as Washington, Lee and Sherman who saw and spoke against the waste and cruelty of war.

INDEX

147

148

149